Dictionary of
Irish Quotations

Dictionary of Irish Quotations

Sean Sheehan

MERCIER PRESS

MERCIER PRESS

Trade enquiries to CMD DISTRIBUTION,
55a Spruce Avenue, Stillorgan Industrial Park, Blackrock, Dublin

© Sean Sheehan 1993

ISBN 1 85635 052 5

A CIP is available of this book from the British Library.

First published in 1993
10 9 8 7 6 5

Cover images courtesy of the National Library of Ireland, National
Photographic Archive, The Pearse Museum, Kilmainham Gaol and Photocall

Printed in Ireland by Colour Books Ltd.

Contents

Introduction

This small volume does not set out to be a comprehensive dictionary of Irish quotations; rather is it a modest collection of interesting – and sometimes just witty – remarks made by Irish people on a number of topical subjects.

Quotations, by definition, are taken out of context and so a fuller appreciation of the author's meaning can only be enjoyed by returning to the source of the remark. Maria Edgeworth's scathing description of those who use too many quotations as a substitute for genuine knowledge serves as a warning. 'The everlasting quotation-lover dotes on the husks of learning,' she advised, and went on to characterise such a person as '... a bore in second childishness'. But being senile is not a prerequisite for occasionally dipping into this *Dictionary of Irish Quotations*. It is more comfortable to remember what a character said in Benedict Kiely's novel, *Nothing Happens in Carmincross*: 'Every quotation is a renewed experience, a light switched on again in a darkened room to reveal familiar objects'.

What makes a quotation an Irish one? The obvious answer – one where the author is Irish – only begs the question, given the slippery nature of an Irish identity. The comedian Sean Hughes, who is included here, was born in London, but of Irish parents who returned to Dublin with him when he was five. His humour, as he says himself, stems from a Catholic self-hatred, and he seems far more Irish than someone like Iris Murdoch – who is not included – who may have been born in Ireland but whose writing has all the hallmarks of being essentially English. Jonathan Swift, on the other hand, was born in Ireland but seemed to resent the fact: 'As to my native country,' he claimed, 'I happened indeed by a perfect accident to be born here, my mother being left here from returning to her house at Leicester....' Yet, despite such mis-givings, he spent most of his life in the country and many characteristics of his style are quintessentially Irish.

Given the Irish diaspora, it would be easy to extend the notion of Irishness to quotable people from many parts of the world but this collection contents itself with authors born or brought up in the country. 'Irish Americans are about as Irish as Black Americans are African,' declared Bob Geldof – and he has a point. To complicate matters, it is also true that some people born and living in Ireland prefer to think of themselves as British; but they have not been excluded from this collection.

However, discussion about Irishness can easily become sterile and divisive and it is easy to fall into a gentle racism that would award the Irish some natural copyright for quotations, on the grounds of an innate disposition to make clever and pithy re-marks. Such an apparent insight into the national character has been alleged too often, both as a form of self-congratulation and as a source for satire by others. It is more stimulating to stress the healthy diversity of opinions and attitudes to be found in this collection. Definitions of nationality are less interesting and enter-taining than a pluralism of thought, and seeking a miscellany has been the purpose of this book. 'I have no views to inter,' as Samuel Beckett remarked when explaining his refusal to give an interview.

Quotations

Appearances

* There is no trusting appearances.
    Richard Brinsley Sheridan (1751–1816): *The School for Scandal*

* We cannot judge either of the feelings or of the characters of men with perfect accuracy, from their actions or their appearance in public; it is from their careless conversations, their half-finished sentences, that we may hope with the greatest probability of success to discover their real character.
    Maria Edgeworth (1767–1849): *Castle Rackrent*

* Oh, think not my spirits are always as light,
    And as free from a pang as they seem to you now.
    Thomas Moore (1779–1852): *Irish Melodies*

* It is only shallow people who do not judge by appearances.
    Oscar Wilde (1854–1900): *The Picture of Dorian Gray*

* Being natural is only a pose, and the most irritating pose I know.
    Oscar Wilde (1854–1900): *The Picture of Dorian Gray*

* A well-tied tie is the first serious step in life.
  Oscar Wilde (1854–1900): *The Importance of Being Earnest*

* All great truths begin as blasphemies.
  George Bernard Shaw (1856–1950): *Annajanska*

* Never mind about my soul, just make sure you get my tie right.
  James Joyce (1882–1941): [Responding to the painter Patrick Tuohy's assertion that he wanted to capture Joyce's soul in his portrait]

* I have always felt that everybody on earth goes about in disguise.
  Seán O'Faolain (1900–1991): *What it feels like to be a Writer*

* The city dweller who passes through a country town, and imagines it sleepy and apathetic is very far from the truth: it is watchful as the jungle.
  John Broderick (1927–): *The Pilgrimage*

***

Art

* When once the itch of literature comes over a man, nothing can cure it but the scratching of a pen.
  Samuel Lover (1797–1868): *Handy Andy*

* You may grind their souls in the self-same mill,
  You may bind them, heart and brow;
  But the poet will follow the rainbow still,
  And his brother will follow the plough.
  John Boyle O'Reilly (1844–90): 'The Rainbow's Treasure'

* All art is quite useless.
                    Oscar Wilde (1854–1900): *The Picture of Dorian Gray*

* But my work is undistinguished
  And my royalties are lean
  Because I never am obscure
  And not at all obscene.
                    Michael MacManus (1888–1951): 'An Author's Lament'

* Sure, 'tis God's ways is very quare,
  An' far beyont my ken,
  How o' the self same clay he makes
  Poets an' useful men.
                    Agnes Kendrick Gray (1894–?): 'The Shepherd to the Poet'

* The artist, like the God of the creation, remains within or
  behind or beyond or above his handiwork, invisible, re-
  fined out of existence, indifferent, paring his fingernails.
       James Joyce (1882–1941): *A Portrait of the Artist as a Young Man*

* It is a symbol of Irish art. The cracked lookingglass of a
  servant.
                    James Joyce (1882–1941): *Ulysses*

* Is there something paralysingly holy in the vicious nature
  of the word that is not found in the elements of the other
  arts? Is there any reason why that terrible materiality of
  the word surface should not be capable of being dissolved,
  like for example the sound surface, torn by enormous
  pauses, of Beethoven's Seventh Symphony, so that
  through whole pages we can perceive nothing but a path
  of sounds suspended in giddy heights, linking unfathom-
  able abysses of silence?
                    Samuel Beckett (1906–89): [Letter to Axel Kaun]

* His writing is not *about* something; it is that something
  itself.
                    Samuel Beckett (1906–89): In *Our Exagmination Round His
                    Factification For Incamination of 'Work in Progress'*

* The hell of it seems to be, when an artist starts saving the world, he starts losing himself.

    Brian Friel (1929–): *Extracts from a Sporadic Diary*

* Between my finger and my thumb
  The squat pen rests.
  I'll dig with it.

    Seamus Heaney (1939–): 'Digging'

* The writers of the revivalist generation believed that it was the artist's duty to insult, as well as occasionally to flatter, his fellow-countrymen; and Yeats spoke for many when he said that a man of real genius is never like a country's idea of itself. But modern Irish artists seem all too like the more conventional bards of Classical Ireland – all too willing to reflect rather than to interrogate current state policy. Within the past generation, there has been a massive change. Not long ago, artists and intellectuals were oppressed by the Irish people; but now, there is a distinct possibility that the Irish people are oppressed – in the sense of misrepresented or ignored – by the intellectuals.

    Declan Kiberd (1951–): *Irish Literature & Irish History*

***

Capitalism

* Whenever the workers challenged the interests of capital they found themselves confronted by the fact that the employers had influence in making the laws while they had none. New restrictions, new penal laws, more barbarous and absurd than the preceding, are enacted; the producers take measures to defeat these iniquitous laws; they endeavour by a counterforce to make head against the violences instituted against them; they resort to plots and combinations of violence to defeat the power which

seeks under the name of law to repress for ever their spirit, and with it their industry. They endeavour by unjust violence towards their own number and sullen threats against their employers to keep down the depressing competition of low wages. Thus is a community converted into a theatre of war: hostile camps of the employers and labourers are everywhere formed.

William Thompson (1785–1833): *An Inquiry into the Principles of the Distribution of Wealth most Conducive to Human Happiness*

* There's a proud array of soldiers–
  what do they round your door?
  They guard our master's granaries
  from the thin hands of the poor.

  Lady Jane Wilde (1826–96): 'The Famine Years'

* In a community like ours, where property confers immense distinction, social position, honour, respect, titles, and other pleasant things of the kind, man being naturally ambitious, makes it his aim to accumulate this property, and goes on wearily and tediously accumulating it long after he has got more than he wants, or can use, or enjoy, or perhaps even know of. Man will kill himself by overwork in order to secure property, and really, considering the enormous advantages that property brings, one is hardly surprised.

  Oscar Wilde (1854–1900): *The Soul of Man Under Socialism*

* Property is organised robbery.

  George Bernard Shaw (1856–1950): Preface to *Major Barbara*

* To me judges seem the well paid watch-dogs of Capitalism, making things safe and easy for the devil Mammon.

  Maud Gonne (1866–1953): [Letter to Yeats]

* Governments in a capitalist society are but committees of the rich to manage the affairs of the capitalist class.

  James Connolly (1868–1916): [*Irish Worker*, August 1914]

*   But who are the Irish? Not the rack-renting, slum-owning
     landlord; not the sweating, profit-grinding capitalist; not
     the sleek and oily lawyer; not the prostitute pressman –
     the hired liars of the enemy. Not these are the Irish upon
     whom the future depends.

     James Connolly (1868–1916): *The Irish Flag*

*   'Do you know the difference between having an Irish
     Republic and being a section of the British Empire?' my
     granny often asked me.
     'No,' says I, 'what is it?'
     'From one you'll get an eviction order written in English
     with the lion and the unicorn, and from the other an evic-
     tion order written in Irish with a harp.'

     Brendan Behan (1923–64): [Quoted in *The Wit of Brendan Behan*
     compiled by Sean McCann]

                              ***

Catholicism

*   Jew, Turk or atheist
     May enter here, but not a papist.
                    *
     Whoever wrote this wrote it well
     For the same is written in the gates of Hell.
                    Anonymous (17th century): [Notice on the walls of Bandon
                    town and the reply that appeared afterwards]

*   Your priests, whate'er their gentle shamming,
     Have always had a taste for damning.
                    Thomas Moore (1779–1852): *Twopenny Post-Bag*

*   Hell is not hot enough, nor eternity long enough, to punish these miscreants.

> Bishop David Moriarty of Kerry (1814–77): [Expressing the
> Catholic Church's response to the Fenians in 1867]

* The time has long since gone when Irish men and Irish
women could be kept from thinking by hurling priestly
thunder at their heads.

> James Connolly (1868–1916): *Labour, Nationality and Religion*

* Stately, plump Buck Mulligan came from the stairhead,
bearing a bowl of lather on which a mirror and a razor lay
crossed. A yellow dressinggown, ungirdled, was sustain-
ed gently behind him by the mild morning air. He held the
bowl aloft and intoned:
–*Introibo ad altare Dei.*

> James Joyce (1882–1941): *Ulysses*

* I was liberated but not too liberated. I was Catholic, you
see, and my conscience always bothered me.

> Eileen O'Casey (1905–): [*Los Angeles Times*, 15 November 1974]

* No one can seriously doubt but that the Catholic Church
has behaved to all our political parties in an identical way
as the Orange Order in its control of the Unionist Party in
the North – a sectarian and bigoted politically conservative pressure group.

> Noel Browne (1915–): [*The Irish Times*, 1 May 1971]

* The Roman Catholic Church is getting nearer to communism every day.

> Ian Paisley (1926–): [*The Irish Times*, 13 September 1969]

* A tribe of witch-doctors in black exerting what they call
their God-given authority, encouraging superstition and
observances instead of true religion which if it happened
to catch on might make them redundant.

> Francis Stuart (1902–): 'An Abandoned Snail Shell'

*   Among the best traitors Ireland has ever had, Mother
Church ranks at the very top, a massive obstacle in the
path to equality and freedom.

> Bernadette Devlin (1947–): *The Price of My Soul*

*   Intellectually I resisted, but though logic stripped away
the cant and ceremony I still could not rid myself of the
voodoo.

> Bob Geldof (1952–): *Is That It?*

*   Fight the real enemy.

> Sinéad O'Connor (1966–): [On a US television show in 1992,
> as she tore up a picture of the Pope]

***

Childhood

*   I'll tell my ma when I go home,
The boys won't leave the girls alone,
They pull my hair, they stole my comb.
But that's all right till I go home.
She is handsome, she is pretty,
She is the belle of Belfast city,
She is courtin' one, two, three,
Please won't you tell me who is she?

> Anonymous (20th century): 'I'll Tell My Ma'

*   We must be content to begin at the beginning, if we would
learn the history of our own mind; we must condescend to
be even as little children, if we would discover or recollect
those small causes which early influenced the imagination,
and afterward became strong habits, prejudices, and passions.

> Maria Edgeworth (1767–1849): *Harrington*

* In ancient shadows and twilights
  Where childhood had strayed
  The world's great sorrows were born
  And its heroes were made.
  In the lost boyhood of Judas
  Christ was betrayed.

  George William Russell (Æ) (1867–1935): 'Germinal'

* Once upon a time and a very good time it was there was a
  moocow coming down along the road and this moocow
  that was down along the road met a nicens little boy
  named baby tuckoo.

  James Joyce (1882–1941): *A Portrait of the Artist as a Young Man*

* Do engine drivers, I wonder, eternally wish they were
  small boys?

  Brian O'Nolan (pseudonym Flann O'Brien, Myles na gCopaleen)
  (1911–66): *The Best of Myles*

* I was 14, and abruptly at the end of the holidays some soft,
  almost physical appendage of childhood seemed to have
  fallen away, like the tail of a tadpole, and I would never be
  quite the same again.

  Val Mulkerns (1925–): *Home for Christmas*

* Adults used to say things to me like, 'How long since I've
  seen you?' and I'd reply, 'Five years'. And they'd say,
  'You have grown'. My mother actually said to me one day
  when I was up a tree, 'Don't climb the tree'. I said 'I am up
  there,' but she said, 'If you fall out of it don't come run-
  ning to me'. I used to ask myself, 'What is she talking
  about?' So I vowed when I grew up I'd never be an adult.

  Dave Allen (1936–): [Television interview, 1987, quoted in
  God's Own Comedian by Gus Smith]

***

Compliments

*   Yet he was kind, or if severe in aught,
The love he bore to learning was at fault.
Oliver Goldsmith (1728–1774): 'The Deserted Village'

*   Won't you come into the garden? I would like my roses to
see you.
Richard Brinsley Sheridan (1751–1816): [To a young lady –
Attributed]

*   Holy Moses! Have a look!
Flesh decayed in every nook.
Some rare bits of brain lie here,
Mortal loads of beef and beer.
Amanda Ros (1860–1939): 'Lines on Westminster Abbey'

*   Swift has sailed into his rest;
Savage indignation there
Cannot lacerate his breast.
Imitate him if you dare,
World-besotted traveller; he
Served human liberty.
W.B. Yeats (1865–1939): 'Swift's Epitaph'

*   'May I kiss the hand that wrote *Ulysses*?'
     [The request of a young admirer to Joyce in Zürich]
'No, it did lots of other things too'.
James Joyce (1882–1941): [Quoted in
Richard Ellmann's biography]

*   Tea with Madam Gonne MacBride … Her heroic and now
cavernous beauty, made sombre by the customary black
draperies she wears, is also illumined by an unceasing
gentleness and humour; she has now what seemed a faint,
far-away amusement at life.
Micheál MacLiammóir: (1899–1978): *Put Money in Thy Purse*

* Samuel Beckett is an old and good friend of mine, he's also
 a marvellous playwright. I don't know what his plays are
 about, but I enjoy them. I don't know what a swim in the
 sea is, but I enjoy the water flowing over me.
>   Brendan Behan (1923–64): [Quoted in *The Wit of Brendan Behan*
>   compiled by Sean McCann]

***

Death

* They brought her to the city
   And she faded slowly there–
 Consumption has no pity
   For blue eyes and golden hair.
>   Richard d'Alton Williams (1822–62): 'The Dying Girl'

* Peace, peace, she cannot hear
   Lyre or sonnet,
 All my life's buried here,
   Heap earth upon it.
>   Oscar Wilde (1854–1900): 'Requiescat'

* Like a bairn to his mither, a wee birdie to its nest,
 I wud fain be ganging nod unto my Saviour's breast;
 For he gathers in his bosom witless, worthless lambs like
>   me,
 An' he carries them himsel' to his ain countree.
>   Mary Lee Demarest (1857–88): 'My Ain Countree'

* Nor law, nor duty bade me fight,
 Nor public man, nor angry crowds,
 A lonely impulse of delight
 Drove to this tumult in the clouds;
 I balanced all, brought all to mind,
 The years to come seemed waste of breath,
 A waste of breath the years behind

In balance with this life, this death.
>   W.B. Yeats (1865–1939): 'An Irish Airman Foresees his Death'

* Nor dread nor hope attend
A dying animal;
A man awaits his end
Dreading and hoping all.
>   W.B. Yeats (1865–1939): 'Death'

* – *I am the resurrection and the life.* That touches a man's inmost heart.
– It does, Mr Bloom said.

    Your heart perhaps but what price the fellow in the six feet by two with his toes to the daisies? No touching that. Seat of the affections. Broken heart. A pump after all, pumping thousands of gallons of blood every day. One fine day it gets bunged up: and there you are. Lots of them lying around here: lungs, hearts, livers. Old rusty pumps: damn the thing else. The resurrection and the life. Once you are dead you are dead. That last day idea. Knocking them all up out of their graves. Come forth, Lazarus! And he came fifth and lost the job. Get up! Last day! Then every fellow mousing around for his liver and his lights and the rest of his traps. Find damn all of himself that morning.
>   James Joyce (1882–1941): *Ulysses*

* Drumm: I asked him if he had the results of the x–rays. He took me into his surgery … He gave me one of those looks of his, redolent of the cemetery, and said that I should buy day-returns from now on instead of season tickets.
>   Hugh Leonard (Pseudonym of John Keyes Byrne) (1926–): *A Life*

* My grandmother made dying her life's work.
>   Hugh Leonard (Pseudonym of John Keyes Byrne) (1926–):
>   *Home Before Night*

* come not with ornate grief
to desecrate my sleep

but a calm togetherness of hands
> Christy Brown (1932–81): 'Come Softly to My Wake'

* '… I *see*,' he said with emphasis, 'the faces of the little children who have lost a father, as they walk behind the coffin
with roses in their hands. I see the faces of good, honest,
decent people who have never done wrong to anyone else,
who have lost a loved one, blown to bits by a terrorist
bomb. And of course I weep.
> Dr Robin Eames (1940–) [Referring to Enniskillen bombing, 8
> November 1987, quoted in *Observer* 12 April 1992]

* People die, no matter how much they are needed. It is possible to live and make effective use of one's life, no matter
how little one may be personally interested in living.
> Bernadette Devlin (1947–): [Interview in *The Sun* newspaper,
> 30 April 1969]

***

Drink

* I should like a great lake of ale
For the King of Kings.
> Brigid of Kildare (453–523): *The Feast of St Brigid of Kildare*

* I have fed purely upon ale; I have eat my ale, drank my
ale, and I always sleep upon ale.
> George Farquhar (1678–1707): *The Beaux' Stratagem*

* O, long life to the man who invinted potheen
Sure the Pope ought to make him a martyr
If myself was this moment Victoria, our Queen
I'd drink nothing but whiskey and wather.
> Zozimus (Pseudonym of Michael Moran) (1794–1846):
> 'In Praise of Potheen'

* I was blue mouldy for the want of that pint. Declare to God I could hear it hit the pit of my stomach with a click.

James Joyce (1882–1941): *Ulysses*

* I only take a drink on two occasions – when I'm thirsty and when I'm not.

Brendan Behan (1923–64): [Quoted in *The Wit of Brendan Behan* compiled by Sean McCann]

* I have made an important discovery ... that alcohol, taken in sufficient quantities, produces all the effects of intoxication.

Oscar Wilde (1854–1900): *In Conversation*

* When things go wrong and will not come right,
Though you do the best you can,
When life looks black as the hour of night–
A PINT OF PLAIN IS YOUR ONLY MAN.

Brian O'Nolan (pseudonym Flann O'Brien, Myles na gCopaleen) (1911–66): *At-Swim-Two-Birds*

* The first double had no effect and neither had the second; the third thawed him; the fourth warmed him; and the fifth lit a taper in his mind that shone on the surrounding dark, colouring it like a winter moon bursting through low cloud. The self-destructive edge vanished from his thoughts, words flowed as bright as spring water, and laughter came easily and without overt reason. Between the fifth and the twelfth double he lived on a plateau of unconsidered pleasure which he tried to prolong until after closing time. The twelfth double was followed by a period of deterioration during which the commonest words seemed like tongue-twisters, and thoughts came slowly like the last drops from a squeezed lemon.

Patrick McGinley (1937–): *Bogmail*

***

Dublin

*   In Dublin's fair city,
       Where the girls are so pretty,
    I first set my eyes on sweet Molly Malone.
                                      Anonymous: 'Cockles and Mussels'

*   Now if you go to the fighting line and there to fight the
                                                    Boer,
    Will you kindly hould the Dublins back, and let the
                                          culchies go before.
                                      Anonymous: 'Get Me Down My Petticoat'

*   The Forces of the Irish Republic which was proclaimed in
    Dublin on Easter Monday, 24 April, have been in posses-
    sion of the central part of the capital since 12 noon on that
    day ... They have redeemed Dublin from many shames
    and made her name splendid among the names of cities.
                     Patrick Pearse (1879–1916): [Statement issued from the
                              headquarters of the Easter Rising, 28 April 1916]

*   My intention was to write a chapter of the moral history of
    my country and I chose Dublin for the scene because that
    city seemed to me the centre of paralysis.
        James Joyce (1882–1941): [Letter to Grant Richards, 5 May 1905]

*   Tomatoes, mush-er-rooms, the last of the collies,
    Iceberg leuttice, thirty a head,
    Keukin apples, five for fifty,
    Fresh fleurs.
    Tobler, Tobler, get the big Tobler-owen
    Nointy-noine P,
    Any choc-alet ba-ers, five for a pou-end
    To-bler-owen, get the big Tobler.
                              Street vendors in Henry Street [Quoted in the
                              Ultimate Dublin Guide by Brian Lalor]

* Dublin made me and no little town,
  With the country closing in on its streets
  The cattle walking proudly on its pavements
  The jobbers, the gombeenmen and the cheats
  Devouring the fair-day between them.

  Donagh MacDonagh (1912–68): 'Dublin Made Me'

* Dublin is a state of mind as much as a city.

  Tom MacDonagh (1934–): *My Green Age*

* The Irish are the niggers of Europe ... An' Dubliners are
  the niggers of Ireland ... An' the northside Dubliners are
  the niggers o' Dublin – Say it loud. I'm black an' I'm
  proud.

  Roddy Doyle (1958–): *The Commitments*

***

The English

* The Englishman has all the qualities of a poker except its
  occasional warmth.

  Daniel O'Connell (1775–1847): [Attributed]

* Firm on a rock, a Briton born,
  A foreign coast he views with scorn;
  There 'tween roast beef and porter hung,
  Each sense suspended, but the tongue,
  Free 'midst a load of ills he reigns,
  Tax'd at all points except his brains.

  Mary O'Brien (*flourished* 1783–90): 'The Freedom of John Bull'

* The English have a miraculous power of turning wine into
  water.

  Oscar Wilde (1854–1900): *In Conversation*

* An Englishman does everything on principle: he fights
you on patriotic principles; he robs you on business principles; he enslaves you on imperial principles.
George Bernard Shaw (1856–1950): *The Man of Destiny*

* Englishmen never will be slaves; they are free to do whatever the government and public opinion allow them to do.
George Bernard Shaw (1856–1950): *Man and Superman*

* It has always been very curious to me how Irish sentiment
sticks in this half-way house – how it continues to ap-
parently hate the English and at the same time continues
to imitate them.
Douglas Hyde (1860–1949): 'On the Necessity for
de-Anglicising the Irish People'

* The English always have their wars in someone else's
country.
Brendan Behan (1923–64): [Quoted in *The Wit of Brendan Behan*
compiled by Sean McCann]

* I prefer to live in Ireland, but I've a great admiration for
the British people. No one else could have used Churchill
so well during the war and then thrown him out at the
right time afterwards.
Brendan Behan (1923–64): [Quoted in *The Wit of Brendan Behan*]

* Most people look upon the English as being a very sober
race, but I know a lot of them who, I would say, have a
stiff upper lip mostly because they are 'stiff' twenty-four
hours a day.
Brendan Behan (1923–64): [Quoted in *The Wit of Brendan Behan*]

* If I make a good movie they say I'm a British director and
if I make what they think is a bad one, they say I'm
Irish!
Neil Jordan (1951–): [Interview in *The Independent*, 3 February 1993]

Failure

*   At moments he had fits of depression and melancholy. He
did not wish to be alone. He would often – a most unusual
thing for him – talk for talking's sake. He would walk the
streets of Dublin with a follower far into the night, rather
than sit in his hotel by himself.

R. Barry O'Brien (1847–1918): *The Life of Charles Stewart Parnell*

*   Experience is the name every one gives to their mistakes.

Oscar Wilde (1854–1900): *Lady Windermere's Fan*

*   Now that my ladder's gone
I must lie down where all the ladders start
In the foul rag-and-bone shop of the heart.

W.B. Yeats (1865–1939): *The Circus Animals' Desertion*

*   Do
not remember my failures,
But remember this my faith.

Patrick Pearse (1879–1916): *The Fool*

*   Think – what I have got for Ireland? Something which she
has wanted these past seven hundred years. Will anyone
be satisfied at the bargain? Will anyone? I tell you this –
early this morning I signed my death warrant. I thought at
the time how odd, how ridiculous – a bullet may just as
well have done the job five years ago.

Michael Collins (1890–1922): [To his friend John O'Kane
after signing the Treaty with Britain]

***

The Family

* Forbearance towards errors and defects, and a just appreciation of good qualities, joined to mildness and good breeding, is what we would inculcate as the surest means of preserving domestic harmony, and of promoting domestic affection.

> Marguerite Power, Countess of Blessington (1789–1849):
> *The Repealers*

* The black dog was the only intelligent member of the family. He died a few years later. He was poisoned, and no one will convince me it wasn't suicide.

> Hugh Leonard (Pseudonym of John Keyes Byrne) (1926–): *Da*

***

Fear

* There are many things that we would throw away, if we were not afraid that others might pick them up.

> Oscar Wilde (1854–1900): *The Picture of Dorian Gray*

* Turning and turning in the widening gyre
  The falcon cannot hear the falconer;
  Things fall apart; the centre cannot hold;
  Mere anarchy is loosed upon the world.

> W.B. Yeats (1865–1939): 'The Second Coming'

* I fear those big words, Stephen said, which make us so unhappy.

> James Joyce (1882–1941): *Ulysses*

* I'd take him by the hand and drag him to the window.

Look! There! All that rising corn! And there! Look! The
sails of the herring fleet! All that loveliness! *(Pause)* He'd
snatch away his hand and go back into his corner. Ap-
palled. All he had seen was ashes. *(Pause)* He alone had
been spared. *(Pause)* Forgotten. *(Pause)* It appears the case
is … was not so … so unusual.

Samuel Beckett (1906–89): *Endgame*

*   I am not yet born; Oh fill me
    With strength against those who would freeze my
    humanity, would dragoon me into a lethal automaton,
    would make me a cog in a machine, a thing with
    one face, a thing, and against all those
    who would dissipate my entirety, would
    blow me like thistledown hither and
    thither or hither and thither
    like water held in the
    hands would spill me.
    Let them not make me a stone and let them not spill me,
    Otherwise kill me.

Louis MacNeice (1907–63): 'Prayer Before Birth'

***

Freedom

*   The condition upon which God hath given liberty to man
    is eternal vigilance; which condition if he break, servitude
    is at once the consequence of his crime, and the punish-
    ment of his guilt.

John Philpot Curran (1750–1817): [Speech concerning the election
of the Lord Mayor of Dublin]

*   Liberty, Grace a–vourneen, is just what we imagine of the
    grand ould times in Ireland; it's something that we don't
    quite rightly understand, but which, we believe, must be

all the finer for that.

Marguerite Power, Countess of Blessington (1789–1849):
The Repealers

* The best part of independence, the foundation of every other kind [is] the independence of the mind.

Anna Parnell (1852–1911): *Old Tales and New*

* While to the claims of charity a man may yield and yet be free, to the claims of conformity no man may yield and remain free at all.

Oscar Wilde (1854–1900): *The Soul of Man under Socialism*

* Apostles of Freedom are ever idolised when dead, but crucified when alive.

James Connolly (1868–1916): *Workers Republic*, August 1898

* So that the nation's sovereignty extends not only to all men and women of the nation but to all material possessions of the nation, the nation's soil and all its resources, all wealth and all wealth-producing processes within the nation. In other words, no private right to property is good against the public right to secure strictly equal rights and liberties to every man and woman within the nation.

Patrick Pearse (1879–1916): *The Sovereign People*

* I will not serve that in which I no longer believe whether it call itself my home, my fatherland or my church: and I will try to express myself in some mode of life or art as freely as I can and as wholly as I can, using for my defence the only arms I allow myself to use, silence, exile, and cunning.

James Joyce (1882–1941): *A Portrait of the Artist as a Young Man*

* Is níl laistigh d'aon daoirse
Ach saoirse ó'n daoirse sin.

And only the unfree
Can know what freedom is.

> Seán Ó Ríordáin (1916–77): 'Daoirse' ('Lack of Freedom')

***

Friendship

*   He showed me his bill of fare to tempt me to dine with him; poh, said I, I value not your bill of fare, give me your bill of company.

> Jonathan Swift (1667–1745): *An Argument Against Abolishing Christianity*

*   He cast off his friends as a huntsman his pack,
    For he knew, when he pleased, he could whistle them
    back.

> Oliver Goldsmith (1728–74): *Retaliation*

*   … therefore friends should quarrel to strengthen their attachment, and offend each other for the pleasure of being reconciled.

> Maria Edgeworth (1767–1849): 'An Essay on the Noble Science of Self-Justification'

*   For the poor make no new friends.

> Lady Dufferin (1807–67): 'The Irish Emigrant'

*   Anybody can sympathise with the sufferings of a friend, but it requires a very fine nature to sympathise with a friend's success.

> Oscar Wilde (1854–1900): *The Soul of Man under Socialism*

*   Think where man's glory most begins and ends

And say my glory was I had such friends
     W.B. Yeats (1865–1939): 'The Municipal Gallery Re-visited'

* Greater love than this, he said, no man hath that a man lay
down his wife for his friend. Go thou and do likewise.
Thus, or words to that effect, saith Zarathustra, sometime
regius professor of French letters to the university of Ox-
tail

     James Joyce (1882–1941): *Ulysses*

***

Happiness

* How wide the limits stand
Between a splendid and a happy land!
     Oliver Goldsmith (1728–74): 'The Deserted Village'

* There are some people who cannot be perfectly happy till
they know the *rationale* of their happiness.
     Maria Edgeworth (1767–1849): *Leonara*

* How can we better celebrate our joy – how can we better
fill the measures of our happiness, than by the forgiveness
of our enemies?
     Maria Edgeworth (1767–1849): *Harrington*

* Happiness is a rare plant, that seldom takes root on earth:
few ever enjoyed it, except for a brief period; the search
after it is rarely rewarded by the discovery. But, there is an
admirable substitute for it, which all may hope to attain, as
its attainment depends wholly on self – and that is, a con-
tented spirit.
     Marguerite Power, Countess of Blessington (1789–1849):
     The Victims of Society

* His blissful soul was in Heaven, though a breathing man
                                                    was he;
He was out of time's dominion, so far as the living may be.
                                William Allingham (1824–89): *Poems*

* The fair girl went on her knees and bent over me, fairly
gloating. There was a deliberate voluptuousness which
was both thrilling and repulsive, and as she arched her
neck she actually licked her lips like an animal, till I could
see in the moonlight the moisture shining on the scarlet
lips and on the red tongue as it lapped the white sharp
teeth. Lower and lower went her head as the lips went
below the range of my mouth and chin and seemed about
to fasten on my throat. Then she paused, and I could hear
the churning sound of her tongue as it licked her teeth and
lips, and could feel the hot breath on my neck. Then the
skin of my throat began to tingle as one's flesh does when
the hand that is to tickle it approaches nearer – nearer. I
could feel the soft, shivering touch of the lips on the super-
sensitive skin of my throat, and the hard dents of two
sharp teeth, just touching, pausing there. I closed my eyes
in a languorous ecstasy and waited – waited with beating
heart.

                                Bram Stoker (1847–1912): *Dracula*

* I will arise and go now, and go to Innisfree,
And a small cabin build there, of clay and wattles made;
Nine bean-rows will I have there, a hive for the honey-bee,
And live alone in the bee-loud glade.

And I shall have some peace there, for peace comes
                                        dropping slow,
Dropping from the veils of the morning to where the
                                        cricket sings;
There midnight's all a glimmer, and moon a purple glow,
And evening full of the linnet's wings.
                        W.B. Yeats (1865–1939): 'The Lake Isle of Innisfree'

* What were all the world's alarms

To mighty Paris when he found
Sleep upon a golden bed
That first night in Helen's arms?

W.B. Yeats (1865–1939): 'Lullaby'

* Would you think Heaven could be so small a thing
As a lit window on the hills at night.

Helen Jane Waddell (1889–1965): 'I Shall Not Go To Heaven'

* Dodds: The result is that people with a culture of pov-
erty suffer much less repression than we of the
middle-class suffer and indeed, if I may make
the suggestion with due qualification, they often
have a lot more fun than we have.

Brian Friel (1929–): *The Freedom of the City*

* You can't go back. Only fools go back. The thing is to
grow, and be happy with the way you are growing. All of
us look up at the sky when we're born and plan one day to
reach it. But most give up. They content themselves with
standing higher than their neighbour's roof. They forget
about the sky they once so desperately wanted to touch.
Me, I never want to forget.

Richard Harris (1930–): [Interview, quoted in *Richard Harris, A
Sporting Life* by Michael Feeney Callan]

* When they saw us the crowd erupted, it was a roar like a
football crowd. There were crash barriers out, and beyond
them thousands of heads bobbing up and down, cheering
and throwing their arms up. There was a building site
opposite and all the workers were waving their hard hats.
Passers-by were being caught up in it. I felt the rush of
happiness and warmth coming out of the people and I was
carried out among them on a surge of joy. I suppose when
you die and go to heaven you get a feeling like that.

Gerry Conlon (1954–): *Proved Innocence*

***

Heroes

*   Strange fate of heroes, who like comets blaze,
    And with a sudden light the world amaze;
    But when, with fading beams, they quit the skies,
    No more to shine the wonder of our eyes,
    Their glories spent and all their fiery store,
    We scorn the omens which we feared before.
                Jonathan Swift (1667–1745): 'The Swan Tripe Club in Dublin'

*   I have met them at close of day
    Coming with vivid faces
    From counter or desk among grey
    Eighteenth-century houses.
    I have passed with a nod of the head
    Or polite meaningless words,
    Or have lingered awhile and said
    Polite meaningless words,
    And thought before I had done
    Of a mocking tale or a gibe
    To please a companion
    Around the fire at the club.
                                W.B. Yeats (1865–1939): 'Easter, 1916'

*   Walking to Vespers in my Jesuit school,
    The sky was come and gone: 'O Captain, my Captain!'
    Walt Whitman was the lesson that afternoon –
    How sometimes death magnifies him who dies,
    And some, though mortal, have achieved their race.
                    Denis Devlin (1908–59): 'The Tomb of Michael Collins'

*   We loved you, horseman of the white cockade,
    Above all, for your last words, 'Would to God
    This wound had been for Ireland.' Cavalier,
    You feathered with the wild geese our despair.
                    Richard Murphy (1927–): 'Patrick Sarsfield's Portrait'

*   The great national monuments of Ireland are dead heroes

– preferably those who died young, unfulfilled and beautiful, leaving legend and inspiration behind, but rarely tangible improvements in the lot of those they inspired; and if such a hero left a young girl bereft, *intacta* and keening behind him, so much the better for a sad song.

Polly Devlin (1944–): *All of Us There*

***

Imagination

* I perfectly agree with you in considering castles in the air as more useful edifices than they are generally allowed to be. It is only plodding matter-of-fact dullness that cannot comprehend their use.

Elizabeth Hamilton (1758–1816): *Imagination*

* Imagination, which is the eldorado of the poet and of the novel-writer, often proves the most pernicious gift to the individuals who comprise the talkers instead of the writers in society.

Marguerite Power, Countess of Blessington (1789–1849):
The Repealers

***

Insults

* Like the silver plate on a coffin.

John Philpot Curran (1750–1817): [Describing the smile
of Sir Robert Peel]

* That old yahoo George Moore … His stories impressed me as being on the whole like gruel spooned up off a dirty floor.

Jane Barlow (1857–1917): [Letter, 1914]

* Beneath me here in stinking clumps
  Lies Lawyer Largebones all in lumps;
  A rotten mass of clockholed clay,
  Which grows more honeycombed each day.
  Amanda Ros: (1860–1939) 'Epitaph on Largebones'

* Lord, confound this surly sister,
  Blight her brow with blotch and blister,
  Cramp her larynx, lung, and liver,
  In her guts a galling give her.
  J.M. Synge (1871–1909): [To the sister of a critic of
The Playboy of the Western World]

* English literature's performing flea.
  Sean O'Casey (1880–1964): [Referring to P.G. Wodehouse]

* 'Socialism is worse than communism. Socialism is a heresy
  of communism. Socialists are a Protestant variety of com-
  munists.'
  [From a priest's sermon in Dingle, Kerry in June 1969, quoted in
States of Ireland by Conor Cruise O'Brien]

* Pat: He was an Anglo-Irishman.
  Meg: In the blessed name of God what's that?
  Pat: A Protestant with a horse.
  Brendan Behan (1923–64): *The Hostage*

* Anyone who comes to Canada should bring his own home
  with him.
  Brendan Behan (1923–64): [Quoted in *The Wit of Brendan Behan*
compiled by Sean McCann]

* Our ancestors cut a civilisation out of the bogs and mead-
  ows of this country while Mr Haughey's ancestors were
  wearing pig-skins and living in caves.
  Ian Paisley (1926–): [Speech in Omagh, 1981, quoted in *Paisley*
by Ed Maloney and Andy Pollak]

* The Gestapo in drag.
  Dave Allen (1936–): [Referring to the nuns who educated him]

* If I had a head like yours, I'd have it circumcised.
>> Dave Allen (1936–): [Television anecdote, quoted in *God's Own Comedian* by Gus Smith]

***

The IRA

* Christ, I'm in the wrong house.
>> IRA gunman: [After shooting an innocent man in Belfast, 11 November 1975, quoted in *Irish Political Quotations* by Conor O'Cleary]

* We accept condemnation and criticism ... from the relatives and friends and from our supporters who have rightly and severely criticised us.
>> IRA statement: [After the fire-bombing of La Mon House in Co. Down, 19 February 1978]

* We will tear out their sentimental, imperialist heart.
>> IRA statement: [After the assassination of Lord Mountbatten, 1 September 1979]

* Who here really believers that we can win the war through the ballot box? But will anyone here object if with a ballot box in this hand and an Armalite in this hand we take power in Ireland
>> Danny Morrison (1950–): [November 1981, Provisional Sinn Féin Conference, quoted in *The Provisional IRA* by Patrick Bishop and Eamonn Mallie]

* Armchair generals who whip up anti-nationalist murder gangs ... cannot expect to remain forever immune from the effects of their evil work.
>> IRA statement: [After the killing of Rev. Robert Bradford, Unionist MP, 1981]

* Today, we were unlucky, but remember, we only have to
be lucky once – you will have to be lucky always.
>IRA statement: [After the bombing of Tory Party Conference at
>Brighton, October 1984]

* This cinema has been commandeered by the Irish Repub-
lican Army for the purpose of holding an Easter com-
memoration for the dead who died for Ireland.
>[Statement flashed on a cinema screen in Falls Rd, Belfast, 1970,
>quoted in *Irish Political Quotations* by Conor O'Cleary]

***

Ireland

* This island is a region of dreams and trifles.
>George Berkeley (1685–1753): *The Querist*

* There is a peculiar lightness in the air in Ireland, which …
brings healing on its wings to the over-excited mind, as
well as to the exhausted body.
>Marguerite Power, Countess of Blessington (1789–1849):
>*The Repealers*

* What Ireland might have been, if wisely school'd I know
not; for too briefly Cromwell ruled.
>William Allingham (1824–89): *Laurence Bloomfield in Ireland*

* Was it for this the wild geese spread
The grey wing upon every tide;
For this that all that blood was shed,
For this Edward FitzGerald died,
And Robert Emmet and Wolfe Tone,
All that delirium of the brave;
Romantic Ireland's dead and gone,

It's with O'Leary in the grave.

W.B. Yeats (1865–1939): 'September, 1913'

* – a land whose countryside would be bright with cosy homesteads, whose fields and villages would be joyous with the sounds of industry, with the romping of sturdy children, the contests of athletic youths and the laughter of comely maidens, whose firesides would be forums for the wisdom of serene old age.

Eamon De Valera (1882–1975): [Radio Broadcast, St Patrick's Day 1943]

* Ireland is the old sow that eats her farrow.

James Joyce (1882–1941): *A Portrait of the Artist as a Young Man*

* When the soul of a man is born in this country there are nets flung at it to hold it back from flight. You talk to me of nationality, language, religion. I shall try to fly by those nets.

James Joyce (1882–1941): *A Portrait of the Artist as a Young Man*

* The mountains were thrown higgledy-piggledy into the distance where the sea was. The white dusty road wound round the near flank of the valley and then fell gracefully away to the one-arched bridge below. Among the few tufted oaks beyond the bridge the church lurked. A cluster of thatched houses crouched about it.

Bryan MacMahon (1909–): 'Evening in Ireland'

* The land of scholars and saints:
    Scholars and saints my eye, the land of ambush,
Purblind manifestos, never-ending complaints
    The born martyr and the gallant ninny.

Louis MacNeice (1907–63): *Autumn Journal*

* Ireland is a figment of Anglo-Saxon imagination.

Brendan Behan (1923–64): [Quoted in *The Wit of Brendan Behan* compiled by Sean McCann]

* The problem with Ireland is that it's a country full of genius, but with absolutely no talent.

> Hugh Leonard (Pseudonym of John Keyes Byrne) (1926–):
> [Interview, *The Times* 17 August 1977]

* I remember arriving home from Balistan last year and feeling that I'd come from the Third World to some dotty Fourth World consisting only of Ireland

> Dervla Murphy(1931–): *A Place Apart*

* There are no overall certitudes in Ireland any more. There's a lot of diversity of thinking, a lot of uncertainty, a lot of trying to assimilate to other cultures. It's a time when we need to take stock, to look into our hearts and find a sense of Irishness, to find a pride in ourselves that will make us sure of what we are.

> Mary Robinson (1944–): [Presidential campaign, 1990]

***

The Irish

* *Hibernicis ipsis Hibernior.*

   More Irish than the Irish.

> Anonymous (7th to 9th century)

* Sir Walter Scott once said to me, 'Do explain to the public why Pat, who gets forward so well in other countries, is so miserable in his own.' A very difficult question: I fear above my power. But I shall think of it continually, and listen, and look, and read.

> Maria Edgeworth (1767–1849): [Letter to Michael Pakenham Edgeworth]

* … the Celtic temperament leaps to the weight of a feather; and you have sullen depression, or irresponsible gaiety,

murderous disloyalty or more than feudal fealty, in swift and sudden alterations.

Patrick Augustine (Canon) Sheehan (1852–1913): *Glenanaar*

* We are one of the great stocks of Europe. We are the people of Burke; we are the people of Grattan; we are the people of Swift, the people of Emmet, the people of Parnell. We have created most of the modern literature of this country. We have created the best of its political intelligence.

W.B. Yeats (1865–1939): [Senate Debate, 11 June 1925]

* Deferential to a stranger, they evoked in themselves a sympathetic mood, changing gears in conversation to suit his beliefs and half believing them through sympathy whilst he was present. Afterwards when they checked up on themselves it might be different; they would laugh at the stranger's outlandish opinions when their mood had hardened.

Ernest O'Malley (1898–1957): *On Another Man's Wound*

* Other people have a nationality. The Irish and the Jews have a psychosis.

Brendan Behan (1923–64): *Richard's Cork Leg*

* Yolland: Poteen–poteen–poteen. Even if I did speak Irish I'd always be an outsider here, wouldn't I? I may learn the password but the language of the tribe will always elude me, won't it? The private core will always be ... hermetic, won't it?

Brian Friel (1929–): *Translations*

* Attitudes don't change, the psyche of a country is not changed by wealth, change is not about getting milking machines ... the Irish still feed off the human weaknesses and failures of others.

Edna O'Brien (1932–): [Interview, *The Irish Times*, 12 September 1992]

* The foreman says, 'You must have an intelligence test'. The Irishman says, 'All right.' So the foreman says, 'What is the difference between joist and girder?' And the Irishman says, 'Joyce wrote *Ulysses* and Goethe wrote *Faust*.'
    Dave Allen (1936–): [Retelling the only Irish joke he really liked, quoted in *God's Own Comedian* by Gus Smith]

* Imagine how they stood there, what they stood with that their possessions may become our power.

    Cardboard. Iron. Their hardships parcelled in them.
    Eavan Boland (1944–): 'The Emigrant Irish'

***

Irish History

* Immense and countless was the loss in that place; for the prowess and valour, prosperity and affluence, nobleness and chivalry, dignity and renown, bravery and protection, devotion and pure religion, of the Island, were lost in this engagement.
    Annals of the Four Masters: [Battle of Kinsale, 1601]

* … families, when all was eaten and no hope left, took their last look at the Sun, built up their cottage doors, that none might see them die nor hear their groans, and were found weeks afterwards, skeletons on their own hearth.
    John Mitchel (1815–75): *Jail Journal*

* Lawlessness and turbulence, robbery and oppression, hatred and revenge, blind selfishness everywhere – no principle, no heroism.
    William Allingham (1824–89): *A Diary*

* The Irish Republic is entitled to, and hereby claims, the allegiance of every Irishman and Irishwoman. The Republic guarantees religious and civil liberty, equal rights and

equal opportunities to all its citizens, and declares its re-
solve to pursue the happiness and prosperity of the whole
nation and of all its parts, cherishing all the children of the
nation equally, and oblivious of the differences carefully
fostered by an alien government, which have divided a
minority from the majority in the past.

> Proclamation of the Irish Republic: [Easter 1916]

* And what if excess of love
Bewildered them till they died?
I write it out in a verse –
MacDonagh and MacBride
And Connolly and Pearse
Now and in time to be,
Wherever green is worn,
All changed, changed utterly:
A terrible beauty is born.

> W.B. Yeats (1865–1939): 'Easter, 1916'

* Yeats' *Terrible Beauty* truly has become a sick and sectarian, angry and repressive old crone.

> Noel Browne (1915–): [*The Irish Times*, 23 December 1972]

* Rory O'Connor and Mellows in seizing the Four Courts
were merely echoing Patrick Pearse and the seizure of the
Post Office, and Michael Collins, who could so easily have
starved them out with a few pickets, imitated the English
pattern by blasting the Four Courts with borrowed artillery. And what neither group saw was that every word we
said, every act we committed, was a destruction of the
improvisation and what we were bringing about was a
new Establishment of Church and State in which imagination would play no part, and young men and women
would emigrate to the ends of the earth, not because the
country was poor, but because it was mediocre.

> Frank O'Connor (1903–66): *An Only Child*

* Griffith, Connolly, Collins, where have they brought us?
Ourselves alone! Let the round tower stand aloof

In a world of bursting mortar.

Louis MacNeice (1907–63): 'Autumn Journal'

* The theories of revolution, the theories of nationality, the theories of history, which have brought Ireland to its present pass, cry out for re-examination, and the time is ripe to break with the great enchantment which for too long has made myth so much more congenial than reality.

F.S.L. Lyons (1923–83): *The Meaning of Independence*

* Ireland has been brought to its present pass (that is, the violent chaos in Northern Ireland and its spillovers), not by Britain's conniving with the Ulster Unionist rebellion of 1912 and ignoring the will of most of the people of Ireland, but particularly of the Nationalist Irish in the Six Counties; nor by the scandalous 50 years of British rule in Northern Ireland; nor again by the continuing refusal of Britain, even in 1971, to recognise the Irish nation and its rights there. No, we are told, Ireland has been brought to its present pass in the North by theories of revolution, of nationality, and of history, which we Irish had entertained and must now re-examine; the dire situation has been caused, in other words, by *ourselves*, by the ideas and convictions inspiring our freedom struggle, by our nationalism. The cause of the present evil was not the wrong mind and action of British imperialist nationalism, but the wrong ideas and action of our liberationist nationalism.

Desmond Fennell (1929–): *The Revision of Irish Nationalism*

* The past, implausible and profitless,
Is yet a part of us, though I suppose
Gide has the right of it: who have no sense
Of their own history know most happiness.

Anthony Cronin (1926–): 'Responsibilities'

* There is the squeeze of pain in every episode [of Irish history], and although people sometimes say that the Irish are great lickers of wounds, they have had many to lick.

Polly Devlin (1944–): *All of Us There*

Irish Language

* In the bolder species of composition it is distinguished by a freedom of expression, a sublime dignity, and rapid energy, which it is scarcely possible for any translation fully to convey ... One compound epithet must often be translated by two lines of English verse, and, on such occasions, much of the beauty is necessarily lost; the force and effect of the thoughts being weakened by too slow an introduction on the mind; just as that light which dazzles, when flashing swiftly on the eye, will be gazed at with indifference, if let in by degrees.

  Charlotte Brooke (1740–93): Preface, *Reliques of Irish Poetry*

* To lose your native tongue, and learn that of an alien, is the worst badge of conquest – it is the chain of the soul. To have lost entirely the national language is death; the fetter has worn through.

  Thomas Davis (1814–45): 'The National Language'

* In order to de-Anglicise ourselves, we must at once arrest the decay of the language. We must bring pressure upon our politicians not to snuff it out by their racist discouragement merely because they do not happen themselves to understand it. We must arouse some spark of patriotic inspiration among the peasantry who still use the language, and put an end to the shameful state of feeling – a thousand-tongued reproach to our leaders and statesmen – which makes young men and women blush and hang their heads when overheard speaking their own language.

  Douglas Hyde (1860–1949): 'On the Necessity for De-Anglicising Ireland'

* As long as there is English spoken in the home, whatever is taught in the morning will be undone in the evening by the parents, and the greatest enthusiast has not suggested the shooting of mothers of English-speaking children.

  Oliver St John Gogarty (1878–1957): [On the Gaeltacht Commission Report in the Senate, 10 March 1927]

* To part with it would be to abandon a great part of ourselves, to lose the key of our past, to cut away the roots
from the tree. With the language gone we could never as-
pire again to being more than half a nation.

> Eamon De Valera (1882–1975): [Radio Broadcast,
> St Patrick's Day, 1943]

* The revivalists do not seek merely to revive a language,
which task would be an objective one, susceptible of scien-
tific planning and accomplishment. They seek to propa-
gate the thesis that to be 'Irish' (through and through) one
must be a very low-grade peasant, with peasant concepts
of virtue, jollity, wealth, success, and 'art'. To be a Gael,
one has to change oneself, clothes, brogue and all, into the
simulacrum of a western farm labourer.

> Brian O'Nolan (pseudonym Flann O'Brien, Myles na gCopaleen)
> (1911–66): *The Best of Myles*

* To call a language dead before it dies
means to bury it alive

> Pearse Hutchinson (1927–): 'The Frost is All Over'

* Hugh: Yes, it is a rich language, Lieutenant, full of the
mythologies of fantasy and hope and self-
deception – a syntax opulent with tomorrows.

> Brian Friel (1929–): *Translations*

* Loyalist leaders who express hostility to the Irish language
are actually denying their own past. Not only is this past
evident in many of their names (for example McCusker
and Maginnis), it is obvious also in the fact that at the
time of the siege of Derry most of the population spoke
Irish.

> Gerry Adams (1948–): *The Politics of Irish Freedom*

***

Last Words

* Would this wound had been for Ireland.
    Patrick Sarsfield (1655?–1693): [On being mortally wounded
                at the battle of Landen in Flanders – Attributed]

* Say, shouldst thou grieve to see my sorrows end?
    Thou know'st a painful pilgrimage I've past;
    And shouldst thou grieve that rest is come at last?
    Rather rejoice to see me shake off life;
    And die as I have liv'd, thy faithful wife.
                Mary Monk (?–1715): [Written on her deathbed at Bath,
                            to her husband in London]

* *Ubi saeva indignatio ulterius cor lacerare nequit.*

    Where fierce indignation can no longer tear his heart.
                Jonathan Swift (1667–1745): [Epitaph]

* I find I am but a bad anatomist.
    Theobald Wolfe Tone (1763–98): [Remark to a doctor after
            cutting his windpipe, mistaking it for his jugular]

* My race is run – the grave opens to receive me, and I sink
    into its bosom. I have but one request to ask at my de-
    parture from this world, it is the charity of its silence. Let
    no man write my epitaph; for as no man who knows my
    motives dares now vindicate them, let not prejudice or
    ignorance asperse them. Let them rest in obscurity and
    peace, my memory be left in oblivion, and my tomb re-
    main uninscribed, until other times and other men can do
    justice to my character. When my country takes her place
    among the nations of the earth, then and not till then, let
    my epitaph be written. I have done.
                Robert Emmet (1778–1803): [Before his execution]

* Be my epitaph writ on my country's mind.
    'He served his country and loved his kind'.
                Thomas Davis (1814–45): 'My Grave'

* Either that wallpaper goes or I do.
Oscar Wilde (1854–1900): [Dying in a Paris bedroom – Attributed]

* I am to be shot at dawn. I am glad I am getting a soldier's death. I feared it might be hanging or imprisonment. I have had enough of jail.
Thomas Clarke (1857–1916): [Letter to his wife]

* It is a strange, strange fate, and now, as I stand face to face with death, I feel just as if they were going to kill a boy. For I feel like a boy – and my hands are so free from blood and my heart always so compassionate and pitiful that I cannot comprehend that anyone wants to hang me.
Roger Casement (1864–1916): [Words found in his prison cell after his death]

* It seems perfectly simple and inevitable, like lying down after a long day's work.
Robert Erskine Childers (1870–1922): [Prison letter to his wife]

* O my God, I offer my pain for Ireland. She is on the rack.
Terence MacSwiney (1879–1920): [Letter from prison]

* The beauty of the world hath made me sad,
This beauty that will pass;
Sometimes my heart hath shaken with great joy
To see a leaping squirrel in a tree,
Or a red lady-bird upon a stalk,
Or little rabbits in a field at evening,
Lit by a slanting sun,
Or some green hill where mountainy man hath sown
And soon will reap, near to the gate of Heaven;
Or children with bare feet upon the sands
Of some ebbed sea, or playing on the streets
Of little towns in Connacht,
Things young and happy.
And then my heart hath told me:
These will pass,

Will pass and change, will die and be no more,
Things bright and green, things young and happy;
And I have gone upon my way
Sorrowful.

> Patrick Pearse (1879–1916): 'The Wayfarer'
> [Written the day before his execution]

* Among the many crimes put down to this damned man is
that he did put pepper in the cat's milk and steal a penny
from a blind man, besides wilfully and feloniously and of
his malice aforethought of smiling derisively at a policeman.

> Kevin Barry (1902–20): [Written on the eve of his execution]

* Thank you, Sister – may you be the mother of a bishop!

> Brendan Behan (1923–64): [Quoted in *The Wit of Brendan Behan*
> compiled by Sean McCann]

* When I die I don't want you attacking no screws. I want
you to start clearing your name. My death's going to clear
your name and when you get your name cleared, you
clear mine.

> Giuseppe Conlon (1923–1980): [To his son Gerry Conlon,
> both in prison]

* … get me one miserly book and try to leave it in: the
Poems of Ethna Carbery – cissy. That's really all I want,
last request as they say. Some ask for cigarettes, others for
blindfolds, yer man asks for Poetry.

> Bobby Sands (1954–1981): [Letter from prison, quoted in
> *Ten Men Dead: The Story of the 1981 Irish Hunger Strike*
> by David Beresford]

* Don't mourn for me now
Don't mourn for me never
I'm going to do nothing
For ever and ever.

> Dave Allen (1936–): [Newspaper interview, stating the words he
> wanted inscribed on his tombstone, quoted in *God's Own
> Comedian* by Gus Smith]

Last Words—fictional

* A terrible beauty is born.

W.B. Yeats (1865–1939): 'Easter 1916'

* Yes, the newspapers were right: snow was general all over Ireland. It was falling on every part of the dark central plain, on the treeless hills, falling softly upon the Bog of Allen and, farther westward, softly falling into the dark mutinous Shannon waves. It was falling, too, upon every part of the lonely churchyard on the hill where Michael Furey lay buried. It lay thickly drifted on the crooked crosses and headstones, on the spears of the little gate, on the barren thorns. His soul swooned slowly as he heard the snow falling faintly through the universe and faintly falling, like the descent of their last end, upon all the living and the dead.

James Joyce (1882–1941): 'The Dead'

* The keys to. Given! A way a lone a last a loved a long the

James Joyce (1882–1941): *Finnegans Wake*

* Then the sniper turned over the dead body and looked in-to his brother's face.

Seán O'Faolain (1900–91): 'The Sniper'

***

Life

* Trí aith in domuin:
  brú mná, úth bó, ness gobann

  Three renewals of the world:
  a woman's belly, a cow's udder, a smith's furnace.

Anonymous (9th century)

* What is the life of man? Is it not to shift from side to side, from sorrow to sorrow? – to button up one cause of vexation and unbutton another.

  Laurence Sterne (1713–68): *Tristram Shandy*

* This life is all chequered with pleasures and woes.

  Thomas Moore (1779–1852): *Irish Melodies*

* One's real life is so often the life that one does not lead.

  Oscar Wilde (1854–1900): 'L'Envoi to Rose-Leaf and Apple-Leaf'

* One can live for years sometimes without living at all, and then all life comes crowding into one single hour.

  Oscar Wilde (1854–1900): *Vera, or The Nihilist*

* The soul is born old but grows young. That is the comedy of life. And the body is born young and grows old. That is life's tragedy.

  Oscar Wilde (1854–1900): *A Woman of No Importance*

* 'Fire, food and clothes are the three needs that bring all the drudgery, Máire.'
  'By my baptism, you can be sure and certain of it,' she said.

  Tomás Ó Criomhtháin (1856–1937): *Island Cross-Talk*

* A grain of dust, blown into a man's eye at a certain moment, may change the course of the world's history, still more easily the course of his own history; so I must be excused for recording similar trifles that shunted my destiny on to new lines.

  George Tyrrell (1861–1909): *Autobiography and Life of George Tyrrell*

*   The years like great black oxen tread the world,
And God the herdsman goads them on behind,
And I am broken by their passing feet.
                    W.B. Yeats (1865–1939): *The Countess Cathleen*

*   Welcome, O life! I go to encounter for the millionth time
the reality of experience and to forge in the smithy of my
soul the uncreated conscience of my race ... Old father, old
artificer, stand me now and ever in good stead.
       James Joyce (1882–1941): *A Portrait of the Artist as a Young Man*

*   Nothing is perfect. There are lumps in it.
                    James Stephens (1882–1950): *The Crock of Gold*

*   That was how his life happened
No mad hooves galloping in the sky,
But the weak, washy way of true tragedy –
A sick horse nosing around the meadow for a clean place
                                            to die.
                    Patrick Kavanagh (1904–67): 'The Great Hunger'

*   Estragon: ... Let's go
      Vladimir: We can't
      Estragon: Why not?
      Vladimir: We're waiting for Godot
                    Samuel Beckett (1906–1989): *Waiting for Godot*

*   Where I am, I don't know, I'll never know, in the silence
you don't know, you must go on, I can't go on, I'll go on.
                    Samuel Beckett (1906–1989): *The Unnamable*

*   World is crazier and more of it than we think,
Incorrigibly plural. I peel and portion
A tangerine and spit the pips and feel
The drunkenness of things being various.
                    Louis MacNeice (1907–63): 'Snow'

* By a high star our course is set
Our end is Life. Put out to sea.

> Louis MacNeice (1907–63): 'Thalassa'

* The dawn was contagious, spreading rapidly about the heavens. Birds were stirring and the great kingly trees were being pleasantly interfered with by the first breezes. My heart was happy and full of zest for high adventure.

> Brian O'Nolan (pseudonym Flann O'Brien, Myles na gCopaleen)
> (1911–66): *The Third Policeman*

* I wonder why dreams must be broken, idylls lost and love forgotten? The transience of life has always exasperated me.

> Beatrice Behan (1921–93): *My Life with Brendan*

***

Loneliness

* I am Ireland:
I am lonelier than the Old Woman of Beare.

> Patrick Pearse (1879–1916): 'I am Ireland'

* Tired of the same faces, side-altars,
  She went to the Carmelite Church
At Johnson's Court, confessed her faults,
  There once a week, purchased
Tea, butter in Chatham St. The pond
  In St Stephen's Green was grand.
She watched the seagulls, ducks, black swan,
  Went home by the 15 tram.

> Austin Clarke (1896–1974): 'Martha Blake at Fifty-One'

* I would be the voyeur of myself. This strategy I employed
  for the rest of my captivity. I allowed myself to do and be
  and say and think and feel all the things that were in me,
  but at the same time could stand outside observing and
  attempting to understand.

  Brian Keenan (1950–): *An Evil Cradling*

* Are you ever sitting at home and feeling good about your-
  self but you're actually feeling that lonely that you check
  to see that the telephone's working?

  Sean Hughes (1966–): (*The Independent*, 10 January, 1993]

***

Love

* Be wise, be wise, and do not try
  How he can court, or you be won;
  For love is but discovery;
  When that is made, the pleasure's done.

  Thomas Southerne (1660–1746): *Sir Anthony Love*

* Love, an' please your Honour, is exactly like war, in this,
  that a soldier, though he has escaped three weeks com-
  plete o' Saturday night, may nevertheless be shot through
  his heart on Sunday morning.

  Laurence Sterne (1713–68): *Tristram Shandy*

* The rose still holds its lovely form,
      The dew still sparkles on the tree,
  But, oh! the smile that gave the charm
      No longer beams for me!

  Mary Balfour (1780–1819): 'The Dew each trembling
  Leaf Inwreath'd'

* Oh, who would not welcome that moment's returning,

When passion first wak'd a new life through his frame,
And his soul, like the wood, that grows precious in
burning,
Gave out all its sweets to love's exquisite flame.
Thomas Moore (1799–1852): 'I Saw from the Beach'

* I know, I ask not, if guilt's in that heart,
But I know that I love thee, whatever thou art.
Thomas Moore (1799–1852): 'Come, Rest in This Bosom'

* Have you ever been in love, me boys
Oh! have you felt the pain,
I'd rather be in jail, I would,
Than be in love again;
Johnny Patterson (1840–89): 'The Garden where
the Praties Grow'

* Two children playing by a stream
Two lovers walking in a dream
A married pair whose dream is o'er,
Two old folks who are quite a bore.
Anna Parnell (1852–1911): 'Love's Four Ages'

* When one is in love one begins to deceive oneself. And
one ends by deceiving others.
Oscar Wilde (1854–1900) *A Woman of No Importance*

* Down by the salley gardens my love and I did meet;
She passed the salley gardens with little snow-white feet.
She bid me take love easy, as the leaves grow on the tree;
But I, being young and foolish, with her would not agree.
In a field by the river my love and I did stand,
And on my leaning shoulder she laid her snow-white
hand.
She bid me take life easy, as the grass grows on the weirs;
But I was young and foolish, and now am full of tears.
W.B. Yeats (1865–1939): 'Down by the Salley Gardens'

* Had I the heavens' embroidered cloths,
Enwrought with golden and silver light,
The blue and the dim and the dark cloths
of night and light and the half-light,
I would spread the cloths under your feet:
But I, being poor, have only my dreams;
I have spread my dreams under your feet;
Tread softly because you tread on my dreams.
W.B. Yeats (1865–1939): 'He Wishes for the Cloths of Heaven'

* Love loves to love love. Nurse loves the new chemist. Constable 14A loves Mary Kelly. Gerty MacDowell loves the boy that has the bicycle. M.B. loves a fair gentleman. Li Chi Han lovey up kissy Cha Pu Chow. Jumbo, the elephant, loves Alice, the elephant.
James Joyce (1882–1941): Ulysses

* Beagbheann ar amhras daoine,
Beagbheann ar chros na sagart
Ar gach ní ach a bheith sínte
Idir tú agus falla –

I care little for people's suspicions,
I care little for priests' prohibitions,
For anything save to lie stretched
Between you and the wall –
Máire Mhac an tSaoi (1922–): 'Ceathrúintí Mháire Ní hÓgáin'
('Mary Hogan's Quatrains')

* But then all love seemed to be blighted in Ireland, in another deadly kind of famine. Even the words used for the progression of courtship and love are diminishing and unsympathetic, and make the whole business of love and tenderness seem pathetic, ridiculous, so that the effects and states of being in love become matters for concealment. The first kindling of sexual interest, the recognition of anyone of the opposite sex as being special, is called 'having a notion of' and is regarded as a foolish state. In-

fatuation, or the bloom state of being-in-love, is called
'astray in the head'.

Polly Devlin (1944–): *All of Us There*

***

Marriage

* I looked forward to proposing to enter a state in which the
whole happiness or misery of life depends on the selection
of the object with whom it is to be shared.

Marguerite Power, Countess of Blessington (1789–1849):
My Second Love

* In married life three is company and two is none.

Oscar Wilde (1854–1900): *The Importance of Being Earnest*

* The real drawback to marriage is that it makes one unselfish. And unselfish people are colourless.

Oscar Wilde (1854–1900): *The Picture of Dorian Gray*

* I'm not in favour of long engagements. They give people
the opportunity of finding out each other's character before marriage, which I think is never advisable.

Oscar Wilde (1854–1900): *The Importance of Being Earnest*

* There's nothing in the world like the devotion of a married
woman. It's a thing no married man knows anything
about.

Oscar Wilde (1854–1900): *Lady Windermere's Fan*

* Those who talk most about the blessings of marriage and
the constancy of its vows are the very people who declare
that if the chain were broken and the prisoners were left
free to choose, the whole social fabric would fly asunder.
You can't have the argument both ways. If the prisoner is

happy, why lock him in? If he is not, why pretend that he is?

> George Bernard Shaw (1856–1950): *Man and Superman*

* Marriage is popular because it combines the maximum of temptation with the maximum of opportunity.

> George Bernard Shaw (1856–1950): *Man and Superman*

* So they were married – to be the more together–
And found they were never again so much together
Divided by the morning tea,
By the evening paper,
By children and tradesmen's bills.

> Louis MacNeice (1907–63): 'Plant and Phantom'

* We do not squabble, fight or have rows. We collect grudges. We're in an arms race, storing up warheads for the domestic Armageddon.

> Hugh Leonard (Pseudonym of John Keyes Byrne) (1926–):
> *Time Was*

* To leave my wife and children for love's sake
and marry you would be a failure of nerve.
I remember love and all that goes to make
the marriage, the affairs, that I deserve.

> James Simmons (1933–): 'The End of the Affair'

***

Memories

* Tears fell from my eyes – yes, weak and foolish as it now appears to me, I wept for my departed youth; and for that beauty of which the faithful mirror too plainly assured me, no remnant existed.

> Marguerite Power, Countess of Blessington (1789–1849):
> *The Confessions of an Elderly Lady*

* Oft, in the stilly night,
    Ere Slumber's chain has bound me,
  Fond Memory brings the light
    Of other days around me;
  The smiles, the tears,
    Of boyhood's years,
  The words of love then spoken;
    The eyes that shone,
  Now dimm'd and gone
    The cheerful hearts now broken!
                    Thomas Moore (1779–1852): 'Oft in the Stilly Night'

* The harp that once through Tara's halls
    The soul of music shed,
  Now hangs as mute on Tara's walls
    As if that soul were fled.
                    Thomas Moore (1779–1852): 'The Harp that Once'

* Four ducks on a pond,
  A grass-bank beyond,
  A blue sky of spring,
  White clouds on the wing:
  What a little thing
  To remember for years –
  To remember with tears!
                    William Allingham: (1824–89): 'Four Ducks on a Pond'

* How many men there are in modern life who would like
  to see their past burning to white ashes before them.
                    Oscar Wilde (1854–1900): *An Ideal Husband*

* Reminiscences make one feel so deliciously aged and sad.
                    George Bernard Shaw (1856–1950): 'The Irrational Knot'

* When you are old and gray and full of sleep,
  And nodding by the fire, take down this book,
  And slowly read and dream of the soft look
  Your eyes had once, and of their shadows deep;

How many loved your moments of glad grace,
And loved your beauty with love false or true,
But one man loved the pilgrim soul in you
And loved the sorrows of your changing face;

And bending down beside the glowing bars
Murmur, a little sadly, how love fled
And paced upon the mountains overhead
And hid his face amid a crowd of stars.

W.B. Yeats (1865–1939): 'When You are Old'

* Some time ago, before the introduction of police, all the people of the islands were as innocent as the people here remain to this day. I have heard that at that time the ruling proprietor and magistrate of the north island used to give any man who had done wrong a letter to a jailer in Galway, and send him off by himself to serve a term of imprisonment.

J.M. Synge (1871–1909): *The Aran Islands*

* I do not think of you lying in the wet clay
of a Monaghan graveyard; I see
You walking down a lane among the poplars
On your way to the station, or happily
Going to second Mass on a summer Sunday–

Patrick Kavanagh (1905–67): 'In Memory of My Mother'

* What did they know about memory? What was it but another name for dry love and barren longing?

Mary Lavin (1912–): 'In the Middle of the Fields'

* Constantly the heart releases
Wild geese to the past
Look, how they circle poignant places.

Thomas Kinsella (1928–): 'A Lady of Quality'

Recall all the dreams

That you once used to know
The things you've forgotten
That took you away
to pastures not greener but meaner.

> Van Morrison (1945–): 'I'm Tired Joey Boy'

***

Metaphysics

*   He had been eight years upon a project for extracting sun-
    beams out of cucumbers, which were to be put into phials
    hermetically sealed, and let out to warm the air in raw in-
    clement weather.

> Jonathan Swift (1667–1745): *Gulliver's Travels*

*   All the choir of heaven and furniture of earth – in a word,
    all those bodies which compose the mighty frame of the
    world – have not any subsistence without a mind.

> George Berkeley (1685–1753): *Treatise Concerning the Principles of
> Human Knowledge*

*   Next to me I noticed a tall man seated. He wore a suit of
    navy blue serge. I knew from the way his Adam's apple
    went up and down that he was tall. His moustache was
    golden and his blue eyes were looking straight ahead, fix-
    ed like all Irish eyes on futurity. In my best social accent I
    addressed him. I said, 'It is most extraordinary weather for
    this time of year!' He replied, 'Ah, it isn't this time of year
    at all.'

> Oliver St John Gogarty (1878–1957): *It Isn't This Time
> of Year at All*

*   People who spend most of their natural lives riding iron
    bicycles over the rocky roadsteads of this parish get their
    personalities mixed up with the personalities of their bi-
    cycles as a result of the interchanging of the atoms of each

of them and you would be surprised at the number of people in these parts who nearly are half people and half bicycles.

Brian O'Nolan (pseudonym Flann O'Brien, Myles na gCopaleen) (1911–66): *The Third Policeman*

* So the years hang like old clothes, forgotten in the wardrobe of our minds. Did I wear that? Who was I then?

Brian Moore (1921–): *No Other Life*

***

Money

* Money is the sinews of love, as of war.

George Farquhar (1678–1707): *Love and a Bottle*

* Why spend your leisure bereft of pleasure
    Amassing treasure? Why scrape and save?
Why look so canny at every penny?
    You'll take no money within the grave!
Landlords and gentry, for all their plenty,
    Must still go empty – where'er they're bound:

Riocard Bairéad (1739–1819): 'Another Round'

* A man who knows the price of everything and the value of nothing.

Oscar Wilde (1854–1900): *Lady Windermere's Fan*

* It's a good thing to be able to take up your money in your hand and to think no more of it when it slips away from you than you would of a trout that would slip back into the stream.

Lady Gregory (1859–1932): *Twenty-Five*

*   O you poor folk in cities
A thousand, thousand pities!
Heaping the fairy gold that withers and dies;
One field in June weather
Is worth all the gold that you gather,
One field in June weather – one Paradise.

Katharine Tynan (1861–1931): 'June's Song'

***

Nationalism

*   We soldiers of Erin, so proud of the name,
Will raise upon rebels and Frenchmen our fame;
We'll fight to the last in the honest old cause,
And guard our religion, our freedom, and laws;
We'll fight for our country, our king, and his crown,
And make all the traitors and croppies lie down.

Anonymous: 'Croppies Lie Down'

*   Self-government is our right, a thing born in us at birth, a
thing no more to be doled out to us or withheld from us
by another people than the right to life itself – the right to
feel the sun or smell the flowers, or love our kind. It is
only from the convict these things are withheld, for crime
committed and proven – and Ireland, that has wronged no
man, that has injured no land, that has sought no dominion over others – Ireland is being treated today among the
nations of the world as if she were a convicted criminal.

Roger Casement (1864–1916): [Speech from the Dock]

*   We assert today in this town of Listowel what we asserted
in 1885 and the years before it, that no man has the right to
fix the boundary to the march of a nation – that no man
has a right to limit the aspirations of our people.

Charles Stewart Parnell (1846–91): [Speech in Listowel,
13 September 1891]

* No mouth has the might to set a mearbound to the march
of a landsmaul.

James Joyce (1882–1941): *Finnegans Wake*

* 'What did we get for it? A country, if you'd believe them.
Some of our own johnnies in the top jobs instead of a few
Englishmen. More than half of my own family work in
England. What was it all for? The whole thing was a cod.'

John McGahern (1934–): *Amongst Women*

*   don't be surprised
If I demur, for, be advised
My passport's green.
No glass of ours was ever raised
To toast the Queen.

Seamus Heaney (1939–): *An Open Letter*

* Poetry is defined by its energies and its eloquence, not by
the passport of the poet or the editor; or the name of the
nationality. That way lie all the categories, the separations,
the censorships that poetry exists to dispel.

Eavan Boland (1944–): [Review of Heaney's *An Open Letter*,
The Irish Times, 1 October 1983]

***

The North

* Derry's sons alike defy
Pope, traitor, or pretender
Peal to heaven their 'prentice cry
Their patriot – 'No Surrender!'

Charlotte Elizabeth Tonna (1790–1846): 'No Surrender'

* A culture built upon profit;

Free speech nipped in the bud,
The minority always guilty.
Why should I want to go back
To you, Ireland, my Ireland?
The blots on the page are so black
That they cannot be covered with shamrock.
I hate your grandiose airs,
Your sob-stuff, your laugh and your swagger,
Your assumption that everyone cares
Who is the king of your castle.
Castles are out of date,
The tide flows around the children's sandy fancy.
> Louis MacNeice (1907–63): 'Autumn Journal'

* In my experience, people of Planter stock often suffer from some crisis of identity, of not knowing where they belong. Among us you will find some who call themselves British, some Irish, some Ulstermen, usually with a degree of hesitation or mental fumbling.
> John Hewitt (1907–87): *Collected Poems*

* The national territory consists of the whole island of Ireland, its islands and the territorial seas.
> The Irish Constitution: Article 2

* The great thing I have discovered about Orangemen is that they have feelings.
> Brendan Behan (1923–64): [Quoted in *The Wit of Brendan Behan* compiled by Sean McCann]

* The Catholics have been interfering in Ulster affairs since 1641.
> Ian Paisley (1926–): [*The Irish Times*, 15 August 1968]

* Trusting in the God of our fathers and confident that our cause is just, we will never surrender our heritage.
> Ian Paisley (1926–): [*Guardian*, 21 August 1968]

*   who would connive
in civilised outrage
yet understand the exact
and tribal, intimate revenge.

Seamus Heaney (1939–): 'Punishment'

*   Should I slip away, I wonder,
or go up and touch his shoulder
and talk about the weather

or the price of grass-seed.

Seamus Heaney (1939–): 'The Other Side'

*   Shooting is a popular sport in the countryside ... Unlike
many other countries, the outstanding characteristic of the
sport has been that it is not confined to any one class.
Northern Ireland Tourist Board: [*New Statesman*, 29 August 1969]

*   PARAS THIRTEEN
BOGSIDE NIL.

[Derry graffiti after Bloody Sunday 1972, when thirteen people
died, having been fired on by the British Paratroop regiment]

*   I have a right as the only representative who was a wit-
ness, to ask a question of that murdering hypocrite.

Bernadette Devlin (1947–): [To Reginald Maudling, Home
Secretary, in the House of Commons, 31 January 1972,
quoted in *Irish Political Quotations* by Conor O'Cleary]

*   I am just sorry I did not go for his throat.

Bernadette Devlin (1947–): [To journalists after her attack on the
Home Secretary in the House of Commons, quoted in
Irish Political Quotations by Conor O'Cleary]

*   I have always believed we had a legitimate right to take
up arms and defend our country and ourselves against the
British occupation.

[Falls Road mural, words of Máiréad Farrell, IRA member killed
by the SAS in Gibraltar 1988]

* When you came to this land
  You said you came to understand
  Soldier, we are tired of your understanding.
  Tired of British troops on Irish soil
  Tired of the knock upon the door
  Tired of the rifle butt on the head
  Tired of the jails, the gas, the beatings
  ... Tired of the deaths of our friends
  Tired of the tears and the funerals –
  Those endless endless, funerals.
  ... Is this your understanding?
    Patrick Galvin (1927–): 'Letter to a British Soldier on Irish Soil'

* The two governments ... affirm that any change in the status of Northern Ireland would only come about with the consent of a majority of the people of Northern Ireland.
    Article 1 of Anglo–Irish Agreement, Hillsborough, 1985

* What I cannot get over is that after living there for sixteen years no one said goodbye. On the day we moved out, no one even closed their curtains. Why? I don't really know. I don't think it has much to do with the Anglo–Irish Agreement.
    [A Catholic pressurised into leaving a Protestant area, quoted in
    Guardian, 3 May 1986]

***

Old Age

* When we're worn,
  Hacked hewn with constant service, thrown aside
  To rust in peace, or rot in hospitals.
    Thomas Southerne (1660–1746): *The Loyal Brother*

*   With expectation beating high,
    Myself I now desired to spy;
    And straight I in a glass surveyed
    An antique lady, much decayed.

    Elizabeth Hamilton (1758–1816): [Quoted in *Biography of
    Distinguished Women* by Sarah Hale, 1876]

*   ... it is better to die young than to outlive all one loved,
    and all that rendered one lovable.

    Marguerite Power, Countess of Blessington (1789–1849): *The
    Confessions of an Elderly Gentleman*

*   For ah, my heart! how very soon
    The glittering dreams of youth are past!
    And long before it reach its noon,
    the sun of life is overcast.

    George Moore (1852–1933): 'Elegiac Stanzas'

*   Mrs Allonby: I delight in men over seventy, they always
    offer one the devotion of a lifetime.

    Oscar Wilde (1854–1900): *A Woman of No Importance*

*   The pulse of joy that beats in us at twenty, becomes slug-
    gish. Our limbs fail, our senses rot. We degenerate into
    hideous puppets, haunted by the memory of the passions
    of which we were too much afraid, and the exquisite
    temptations that we had not the courage to yield to.
    Youth! Youth! There is nothing in the world but youth!

    Oscar Wilde (1854–1900): *The Picture of Dorian Gray*

*   What I shall do with this absurdity
    O heart, O troubled heart – this caricature
    Decrepit age that has been tied to me
    As to a dog's tail.

    W.B. Yeats (1865–1939): 'The Tower'

* Oh how you hate old age – well so do I … but I, who am more a rebel against man than you, rebel less against nature, and accept the inevitable and go with it gently into the unknown.

> Maud Gonne (1866–1953): [Letter to W.B. Yeats]

* Seana-bhean isea mise anois, go bhfuil cos léi ins an uaigh is cos eile ar a bruach.

I'm an old woman now, one foot in the grave, and the other on its brink.

> Peig Sayers (1873–1958): *Peig*

* I still think of myself as I was 25 years ago. Then I look in a mirror and see an old bastard and I realise it's me.

> Dave Allen (1936–): [Interview in *The Independent*, 3 March 1993]

***

Optimism

* We are all in the gutter, but some of us are looking at the stars.

> Oscar Wilde (1854–1900): *Lady Windermere's Fan*

* A lament in one ear, maybe; but always a song in the other. And to me life is simply an invitation to live.

> Sean O'Casey (1880–1964): [Quoted in *Eileen* by Eileen O'Casey]

* Run up the sail, my heartsick comrades;
Let each horizon tilt and lurch –
You know the worst; your wills are fickle,
Your values blurred, your hearts impure
And your past life a ruined church…;

> Louis MacNeice (1907–63): 'Thalassa'

* One of the thieves was saved. (Pause) It's a reasonable percentage.

> Samuel Beckett (1907–89): *Waiting for Godot*

* I always carry gelignite; dynamite isn't safe.

> Brendan Behan (1923–64): [Quoted in *The Wit of Brendan Behan* compiled by Sean McCann]

* There is hope for all of us. Well, anyway, if you don't die you live through it, day in, day out.

> Mary Beckett (1926–): *A Belfast Woman*

**

Parents

* I had a good mother, who, when I was a little child, taught me to subdue my own proud spirit, and to be tractable and obedient. Many poor people think that their children will learn this time enough, when they go into the world; and that as they will meet with hardships when they give up, it would be a pity to make them suffer by contradicting them when they are little. But what does a child suffer from correction of a judicious parent, in comparison of what grown people suffer from their passions?

> Elizabeth Hamilton (1758–1816): *The Cottagers of Glenburnie, A Tale for the Farmer's Ingle-nook*

* My mother took too much, a great deal too much, care of me; she over-educated, over-instructed, over-dosed me with premature lessons of prudence: she was so afraid that I should ever do a foolish thing, or not say a wise one, that she prompted my every word, and guided my eyes, hearing with her ears, and judging with her understanding, till, at length, it was found out that I had no eyes, or understanding of my own.

> Maria Edgeworth (1767–1849): *Vivian*

*   Who can speak a mother's anguish?
    Mary Tighe (1772–1810): 'Hagar in the Desert'

*   To lose one parent ... may be regarded as a misfortune; to
    lose both looks like carelessness.
    Oscar Wilde (1854–1900): *The Importance of Being Earnest*

*   Children begin by loving their parents. After a time they
    judge them. Rarely, if ever, do they forgive them.
    Oscar Wilde (1854–1900): *A Woman of No Importance*

*   Parentage is a very important profession but no test of fit-
    ness for it is never imposed in the interest of the children.
    George Bernard Shaw (1856–1950): *Everybody's Political
    What's What*

*   If parents would only realise how they bore their children.
    George Bernard Shaw (1856–1950): *Misalliance*

*   O, father forsaken,
    Forgive your son!
    James Joyce (1882–1941): 'Ecce Puer'

*   There is far greater need for parents to be available to
    their children than previously.
    Bishop Eamonn Casey (1927–): [6 April 1971, quoted in
    Sunday Tribune, 4 September 1992]

*   But today
    It is my father who keeps stumbling
    Behind me, and will not go away.
    Seamus Heaney (1939–): 'Follower'

***

Patriotism

* It is impossible that a man who is false to his friends and neighbours should be true to the public.
    George Berkeley (1685–1753): *Maxims Concerning Patriotism*

* I bear no hate against living thing,
    But I love my country above the King.
    Now, Father, bless me and let me go,
    To die if God has ordained it so.
    William McBurney (1844–92): 'The Croppy Boy'

* Patriotism is the virtue of the vicious.
    Oscar Wilde (1854–1900): *In Conversation*

* You'll never have a quiet world till you knock the patriot-ism out of the human race.
    George Bernard Shaw (1856–1950): *O'Flaherty V.C.*

* What is patriotism but a pure and disinterested philan-thropy, a charity embracing every known and unknown member of the nation's household, and extending to every one of God's creatures, animate and inanimate, which claims with ourselves the motherland as a home.
    Patrick Pearse (1879–1916): [*An Claidheamh Soluis*, 23 December 1905]

* I make no war upon patriotism; never have done. But against the patriotism of capitalism – the patriotism which makes the interest of the capitalist class the supreme test of duty and right – I place the patriotism of the working class, the patriotism which judges every public act by its effect upon the fortunes of those who toil.
    James Connolly (1868–1916): *A Continental Revolution*

* An author's first duty is to let down his country.
    Brendan Behan (1923–64): [Interview in *Guardian*, 15 April 1960]

Pessimism

*   'Do you know what a pessimist is?'
'A man who thinks everybody is as nasty as himself, and
hates them for it.'
George Bernard Shaw (1856–1950): An Unsocial Socialist

*   The whole worl's in a state o' chassis!
Sean O'Casey (1880–1964): Playboy of the Western World

*   All moanday, tearsday, wailsday, thumpsday, frightday,
shatterday till the fear of the Law.
James Joyce (1882–1941): Finnegans Wake

*   Clov: Do you believe in the life to come?
Hamm: Mine was always that.
Samuel Beckett (1906–89): Endgame

*   The sun shone, having no alternative, on the nothing new.
Samuel Beckett (1906–89): Murphy

***

Places

*   There is a green island in lone Gougane Barra
Where Allua of songs rushes forth as an arrow
In deep-valley'd Desmond a thousand wild fountains
Come down to that lake from their home in the
mountains.
Jeremiah Joseph Callanan (1795–1829): 'Gougane Barra'

*   Oh, well I do remember the black December day
The landlord and the sheriff came to drive us all away;
They set my roof on fire with their cursed English spleen,

And that's another reason why I left old Skibbereen.
                              Anonymous (19th century): 'Old Skibbereen'

* And I wished I was in sweet Dungloe and seated on the
                                                    grass,
And by my side a bottle of wine and on my knee a lass,
I'd call for liquor of the best and I'd pay before I would go
And I'd roll my Mary in my arms in the town of sweet
                                                Dungloe.
                              Anonymous (19th century): 'Mary from Dungloe'

* There was an elopement down in Mullingar
But sad to relate the pair didn't get far;
'Oh fly,' said he, 'Darling and see how it feels.'
But the Mullingar heifer was beef to the heels.
                              Anonymous (19th century): 'The Mullingar Heifer'

* Beauing, belle-ing, dancing, drinking,
Breaking windows, damning,
Ever raking, never thinking
Live the rakes of Mallow.
                              Anonymous (19th century): 'The Rakes of Mallow'

* With deep affection and recollection,
I often think of the Shandon bells,
Whose sounds so wild would, in days of childhood,
Fling round my cradle their magic spells.
And this I ponder, where'er I wander,
And thus grow fonder, sweet Cork, of thee.
                    Francis Mahony (pseudonym, Father Prout) (1804–66):
                                              'The Bells of Shandon'

* The light of evening, Lissadell,
Great windows open to the south,
Two girls in silk kimonos, both
Beautiful, one a gazelle.
                    W.B. Yeats (1865–1939): 'In Memory of Eva Gore-Booth and
                                              Con Markiewicz'

*   The brown wind of Connacht –
    Across the bogland blown,
    The brown wind of Connacht
    Turns my heart to stone.
        Anna MacManus (1866–1902): 'The Brown Wind of Connacht'

*   The little waves of Breffney go
    stumbling through my soul.
        Eva Gore-Booth (1870–1926): 'The Little Waves of Breffney'

*   I know a town tormented by the sea
    And there time goes slow
    That the people see it flow and watch it drowsily.
        Mary Davenport (1875–1967): 'Galway'

*   The Donegal border comes so near to Derry city that we
    had only to take the road that runs north and go along it
    for some 20 minutes; then passing a boundary stone we
    knew that we had reached the enchanted ground. Once in
    the territory of the Gael life seemed to hold possibilities
    that were out of question in the realm of Derry of the Lon-
    doners.
        Alice Milligan (1866–1953): *Shan Van Vocht*

*   I am afraid I am more interested, Mr Connolly, in the Dub-
    lin street names than in the riddle of the universe.
        James Joyce (1882–1941): [Remark to Cyril Connolly]

*   To know fully even one field or one lane is a lifetime's
    experience. In the world of poetic experience it is depth
    that counts and not width. A gap in a hedge, a smooth
    rock surfacing a narrow lane, a view of a woody meadow,
    the stream at the junction of four small fields – these are as
    much as a man can fully experience.
      Patrick Kavanagh (1904–67): [Quoted in Introduction to *Contem-
        porary Irish Poetry*, edited by Peter Fallon and Derek Mahon]

*   The names of a land show the heart of the race;
     They move on the tongue like the lilt of a song.
     You say the name and I see the place –
     Drumbo, Dungannon, or Annalong.
     Barony, townland, we cannot go wrong.

     John Hewitt (1907–87): 'Ulster Names'

*   You can leave Killarney behind you, walk along the road
     with the grey wall that hides the beauties of Muckross on
     your right hand, and the moving shoulder of Torc above
     you on the left, up and up until everything touristed and
     ticketed is below in the deep valley, until you feel the
     colour of the mountains, soaking into your eyes, your hair,
     the fragile fabric of skin, until the silence of the high places
     has seeped into your soul.

     Benedict Kiely: (1919–) 'Land Without Stars' in
     Capuchin Annual, 1945/6

*   Old miners at Coalisland
     Going into the ground. Swinging, for
        fear of the gas
     The soft flame of a canary.

     Paul Muldoon (1951–): 'Ma'

                         ***

Politics & Politicians

*   It is a general popular error to suppose the loudest com-
     plainers for the public to be the most anxious for its wel-
     fare.

     Edmund Burke (1729–97): *Observations on the Present State
     of the Nation*

*   He knows nothing; and he thinks he knows everything.
     That points clearly to a political career.

     George Bernard Shaw (1856–1950): *Major Barbara*

*   Politics is the chloroform of the Irish people, or rather the
     hashish.
                    Oliver St John Gogarty (1878–1957): *As I Was Going Down*
                                                        Sackville Street

*   Whenever I wanted to know what the Irish people want-
     ed, I had only to examine my own heart and it told me
     straight off what the Irish people wanted.
                    Eamon De Valera (1882–1975): [Dáil Éireann, 6 January 1922]

*   If I saw Mr Haughey buried at midnight at a cross-roads,
     with a stake driven through his heart – politically speak-
     ing – I should continue to wear a clove of garlic round my
     neck, just in case.
                    Conor Cruise O'Brien (1917–): [*The Observer*, 10 October 1982]

*   I'm not a politician. I've only got one face.
                    Brendan Behan (1923–64): [Quoted in *The Wit of Brendan Behan*
                                              compiled by Sean McCann]

*   There is a cultivated myth that would have us believe that
     De Valera won elections by putting on a big black cloak,
     appearing on platforms at twilight illuminated by blazing
     sods of turf, and casting spells in bad Irish.
                    Breandán Ó hÉithir (1930–90): *Begrudger's Guide to Irish Politics*

*   If John Major was drowning, his whole life would pass in
     front of him and he wouldn't be in it.
                    Dave Allen (1936–): [On stage, 1991, quoted in *The Independent*,
                                                                3 March 1993]

*   Politics can only be a small part of what we are. It's a *way*
     of seeing, it's not all-seeing in itself.
                    Brian Keenan (1950–): *An Evil Cradling*

*   For most people in rural Ireland, political allegiance is a matter of faith, not of belief. It is the allegiance itself, rather than the cause, that is important. The divide of Irish politics, Fine Gael versus Fianna Fáil, has its roots in the civil war, but it is the divide itself, rather than the war, that is the significant element.

John Waters (1955–): *Jiving at the Crossroads*

***

Praise

* Of praise a mere glutton, he swallowed what came,
And the puff of a dunce he mistook it for praise.
Oliver Goldsmith (1728–74): *Retaliation*

* We really are more important than U2 and Sinéad!
Paddy Moloney (1938–): [Quoted in *Irish Rock* by
Tony Clayton-Lea and Richie Taylor]

* Pelé called me the greatest footballer in the world. That is the ultimate salute to my life.
George Best (1946–): *The Good, The Bad and the Bubbly*

***

Regrets

* Nowadays most people die of a sort of creeping common sense, and discover when it is too late that the only things one never regrets are one's mistakes.
Oscar Wilde (1854–1900): *The Picture of Dorian Gray*

* My feet are here on Broadway this blessed harvest morn,

But Oh the ache that's in them for the spot where I was
                                                        born.
My weary hands are blistered from work in cold and heat,
And Oh to swing a scythe to-day, thro' fields of Irish
                                                        wheat.
Had I the chance to wander back, or own a king's abode,
'Tis soon I'd see the hawthorn tree by the Old Bog Road.
                Teresa Brayton (1868–1943) : 'The Old Bog Road'

* O my grief, I've lost him surely. I've lost the only playboy
  of the western world.
                J.M. Synge (1871–1909): *The Playboy of the Western World*

* Too late then, she had found another, moved on. With
  what pain I heard she was seen in a car on the Vico Road.
  A delicate sword thrust through the heart. I hadn't realis-
  ed you had to claim things in this life, it wasn't good
  enough to be well-disposed towards people and things,
  you had to get in there and fight, make a woman aware
  she meant the whole world to you. I was an absolute be-
  ginner in so many ways. Going nowhere.
                Tom MacDonagh (1934–): *My Green Age*

* Oh, shadows of love, inebriations of love, foretastes of
  love, trickles of love, but never yet the one true love.
                Edna O'Brien (1932–): *Night*

                        ***

Religion

* We have just enough religion to make us hate, but not
  enough to make us love one another.
                Jonathan Swift (1667–1745): *Thoughts on Religion*

* I conceive some scattered notions about a superior power
  to be of singular use for the common people, as furnishing

excellent materials to keep children quiet when they grow peevish, and providing topics of amusement in a tedious winter-night.

Jonathan Swift (1667–1745): *An Argument Against Abolishing Christianity*

* Man is by his constitution a religious animal; atheism is against not only our reason, but our instincts.

Edmund Burke (1729–97): *Reflections on the Revolution in France*

* Well! some people talk of morality, and some of religion, but give me a little snug property.

Maria Edgeworth (1767–1849): *The Absentee*

* The rich man in his castle,
The poor man at his gate,
God made them high or lowly,
And ordered their estate.

Cecilia Frances Alexander (1818–95): 'All Things Bright and Beautiful'

* There's no reason to bring religion into it. I think we ought to have as great a regard for religion as we can, so as to keep it out of as many things as possible.

Sean O'Casey (1880–1964): *The Plough and the Stars*

* Let us pray to God ... the bastard! He doesn't exist.

Samuel Beckett (1906–89): *Endgame*

* It's easy to imagine, a god, it's unavoidable, you imagine them, it's easy, the worst is dulled, you doze away, an instant. Yes, God, fomenter of calm, I never believed, not a second.

Samuel Beckett (1906–89): *The Unnamable*

* I'd like to thank God for fucking up my life and at the

same time not existing, quite a special skill.
Sean Hughes (1966–): [*The Independent*, 10 January 1993]

***

Sex

* I have a technical objection to making sexual infatuation a tragic theme. Experience proves that it is only effective in the comic spirit.
George Bernard Shaw (1856–1950): *Three Plays for Puritans*

* What is virtue but the Trades Unionism of the married?
George Bernard Shaw (1856–1950): *Man and Superman*

* … and how he kissed me under the Moorish wall and I thought well as well him as another and then I asked him with my eyes to ask again yes and then he asked me would I yes to say yes my mountain flower and first I put my arms around him yes and drew him down to me so he could feel my breasts all perfume yes and his heart was going like mad and yes I said yes I will Yes.
James Joyce (1882–1941): *Ulysses*

* To her cool mind it had sometimes seemed that the initial expression of tenderness to someone who was – however adored – a stranger, would be difficult to the point of im-possibility. It had never occurred to her that the danger of passion might lie not in its novelty but in its naturalness.
Kate O'Brien (1897–1974): *The Ante-Room*

* During the intervals [between dances] the devil is busy; yes, very busy, as sad experience proves, and on the way home in the small hours of the morning, he is busier still.
[A statmement on all-night dances, by Irish bishops, *Irish Catholic*, 23 December 1933]

*   It's rather like teaching swimming from a book without
     ever having got wet oneself.
> Tim Pat Coogan (1935–): [*Disillusioned Decades,* describing the
> Catholic Church's rulings on matters of sexual morality]

*   Anyone without condoms at the weekend will have to
     wait until Monday.
> [A judge's remark after lifting a fine imposed on a doctor for
> supplying condoms at the weekend when chemists' shops
> were closed. Quoted in *Pro Life?* by Michael Solomon]

*   'My ma discovered I was gay. She was informed by a
     neighbour I was gay. She wasn't sure what that meant but
     contacted the mother of a boy who was known to be gay.
     That woman declared, "Mrs Finucane, don't fret. There
     were always gay men and gay women in Blarney but they
     didn't have the word for it then"'
> Desmond Hogan (1951–): 'The Airedale'

*   Wear one – Just in Casey.
> [Words appearing on T-shirts being sold in Dublin after Bishop
> Casey admitted he had kept secret the fact that he was a father.]

*   If sex is a religion I am an atheist.
> Patrick Healy (1955–): [Interview in *Sunday Independent,*
> 28 February 1993]

***

Shame

*   When lovely woman stoops to folly,
         And finds too late that men betray,
     What charm can soothe her melancholy,
         What art can wash her guilt away?
> Oliver Goldsmith (1728–74): 'The Vicar of Wakefield'

* He does not win who plays with sin
  In the secret House of Shame.
  > Oscar Wilde (1854–1900): 'The Ballad of Reading Gaol'

* We are ashamed of everything that is real about us;
  ashamed of ourselves, of our relatives, of our incomes, of
  our accents, of our opinions, of our experience, just as we
  are ashamed of our naked skins.
  > George Bernard Shaw (1856–1950): *Man and Superman*

* The more things a man is ashamed of, the more respect-
  able he is.
  > George Bernard Shaw (1856–1950): *Man and Superman*

***

Sin

* It has been said that the great events of the world take
  place in the brain. It is in the brain, and the brain only, that
  the great sins of the world take place.
  > Oscar Wilde (1854–1900): *The Picture of Dorian Gray*

* A flushed young man came from a gap of a hedge and
  after him came a young woman with wild nodding daisies
  in her hand. The young man raised his cap abruptly: the
  young woman abruptly bent and with slow care detached
  from her light skirt a clinging twig.

  Father Conmee blessed both gravely and turned a thin
  page of his breviary. *Sin:*
  > James Joyce (1882–1941): *Ulysses*

* The major sin is the sin of being born.
  > Samuel Beckett (1906–1989): *Waiting for Godot*

* Two sins I remember. Once with Kathleen on the clover
  patch of the Fort of Tara. Weary of the warm harvest we
  lay together. Communion bread I ate from the vestry but
  they were unblessed. 'Twas hunger forced me. Fresh are
  the two sins for God to know.

  Joseph Tomelty (1911–): *All Souls' Night*

***

Socialism & Anarchy

* Then raise the scarlet standard high
  Beneath its folds we'll live and die
  Though cowards flinch and traitors sneer
  We'll keep the red flag flying here.

  Jim Connell (1852–1929): 'The Red Flag'

* She [socialism] has the attraction of a wonderful person-
  ality and touches the heart of one and the brain of another,
  and draws this man by his hatred of injustice, and his
  neighbour by his faith in the future, and a third, it may be,
  by his love of art or by his wild worship of a lost and
  buried past. And all of this is well. For, to make men
  Socialists is nothing, but to make Socialism human is a
  great thing.

  Oscar Wilde (1854–1900): [*Pall Mall Gazette*, 15 February 1889]

* If you remove the English army tomorrow and hoist the
  green flag over Dublin Castle, unless you set about the
  organisation of the Socialist Republic your efforts would
  be in vain.

  James Connolly (1868–1916): *Socialism and Nationalism*

* But what is Anarchy? Anarchy means the highest form of
  love. It means that a man must trust himself and live on
  himself ... I am a Socialist. I believe in a co-operative com-

monwealth, but that is far ahead in Ireland.

James Larkin (1876–1947): 'Scathing indictment
of Dublin Sweaters'

* Independence struggles which are led by the conservative
or middle classes, as in Ireland in 1921, tend to compromise with imperialism because their leading sections ben-
efit from such a compromise. That is why those on the left
in Ireland who regard themselves as socialists and as rep-
resentatives of the working class should be the most un-
compromising republicans.

Gerry Adams (1948–): *The Politics of Freedom*

***

Society

* We are all children of our environment – the good no less
than the bad, – products of that particular group of habits,
customs, traditions, ways of looking at things, standards
of right and wrong, which chance has presented to our
still growing and expanding consciousness.

Emily Lawless (1845–1913): *Hurrish*

* Gerald: I suppose Society is wonderfully delight-
ful.
Lord Illingworth: To be in it is merely a bore. To be out of
it is simply a tragedy.

Oscar Wilde (1854–1900):
A Woman of No Importance

* The reasonable man adapts himself to the world: the un-
reasonable one persists in trying to adapt the world to
himself. Therefore all progress depends on the unreason-
able man.

George Bernard Shaw (1856–1950): *Man and Superman*

*   I have a total irreverence for anything connected with
     society except that which makes the roads safer, the beer
     stronger, the food cheaper, the old men and old women
     warmer in the winter and happier in the summer.
                Brendan Behan (1923–64): [Quoted in *The Wit of Brendan Behan*
                                          compiled by Sean McCann]

                                   ***

Sorrow

*   Till Art O'Leary returns
     There will be no end to the grief
     That presses down on my heart,
     Closed up tight and firm
     Like a trunk that is locked
     And the key mislaid.
                Eibhlín Dhubh Ní Chonaill (*c.* 1743–90): 'The Lament for Arthur
                                                          O'Leary'

*   All other things in this sublunary world, fading day by
     day, until nothing of it was left but a tender melancholy,
     like the softened feeling that a summer's twilight produces
     on the mind.
                Marguerite Power, Countess of Blessington (1789–1849):
                                                     My Fourth Love

*   Has sorrow thy young days shaded?
                Thomas Moore (1779–1852): 'Has Sorrow Thy Young'

*   I feel like one
        Who treads alone
     Some banquet-hall deserted,
        Whose lights are fled,
     Whose garlands dead,
        And all but he departed!
                    Thomas Moore (1779–1852): 'Oft in the Stilly Night'

* Where there is sorrow, there is holy ground.
                                    Oscar Wilde (1854–1900): *De Profundis*

***

Time

* He put this engine [a watch] to our ears, which made an incessant noise like that of a water-mill: and we conjecture it is either some unknown animal, or the god that he worships, but we are more inclined to the latter opinion.
                                    Jonathan Swift (1667–1745): *Voyage to Lilliput*

* 'Pleasing for a moment,' said Helen smiling, 'is of some consequence; for, if we take care of the moments, the years will take care of themselves.'
                                    Maria Edgeworth (1767–1849): *Mademoiselle Panache*

* The innocent and the beautiful
  Have no enemy but time.
              W.B. Yeats (1865–1939): 'In Memory of Eva Gore Booth and
                                    Con Markiewicz'

* The train was over half an hour behind its time and the traveller complained to the guard of the train, and the guard spoke to him bitterly. He said, 'You must have a very narrow heart that wouldn't go down to the town and stand your friends a few drinks instead of bothering me to get away'.
                                    Jack B. Yeats (1871–1957): *Sligo*

* The now, the here, through which all future plunges to the past.
                                    James Joyce (1882–1941): *Ulysses*

* Vladimir: That passed the time.

Estragon: It would have passed in any case.
Vladimir: Yes, but not so rapidly.

> Samuel Beckett (1906–89): *Waiting for Godot*

***

Travel

*   I always love to begin a journey on Sundays, because I shall have the prayers of the church, to preserve all that travel by land or by water.

> Jonathan Swift (1667–1745): *Polite Conversation*

*   A man who leaves home to mend himself and others is a philosopher; but he who goes from country to country, guided by the blind impulse of curiosity, is a vagabond.

> Oliver Goldsmith (1728–74): *Citizen of the World, No. 7*

*   Ceo draíochta i gcoim oíche do sheol mé
tré thíorthaibh mar óinmhid ar strae,
gan príomhcharaid díograis im chóngar,
is mé i gcríochaibh tar m'eolas i gcéin;

Through the deep night a magic mist led me
like a simpleton roaming the land,
no friends of my bosom beside me,
an outcast in places unknown

> Eoghan Rua Ó Súilleabháin (1748–84): 'Ceo Draíochta'
> ('Magical Mist')

*   'Tis folly to grieve
For the friends we leave; new lands – new friends we'll

find,

Then away! away!

Is burthen gay;
Let us leave all care behind.

Marguerite Power, Countess of Blessington (1789–1849):
'Flowers of Loveliness'

* Oh, then, fare ye well sweet Donegal, the Rosses and
Gweedore
I'm crossing the main ocean, where the foaming billows
roar.
It breaks my heart from you to part, where I spent many
happy days
Farewell to kind relations, for I'm bound for Amerikay.

Anonymous (19th century): 'Mary from Dungloe'

* A man travels the world over in search of what he needs
and returns home to find it.

George Moore (1852–1933): *Brook Kerith*

* I travel for my turning home
For when I've been six months abroad
Faith your kiss would brighten God!

J. M. Synge (1871–1909): 'Abroad'

* The strands that bind us to our native land are many and
various; we do not admit to ourselves, for we see in them
a sign of weakness, something almost to be ashamed of. It
is only at the odd moment of departure or an unbidden
flash of insight that we realise what love is. As the plane
flies away from home we see in the coastline of Wicklow
the sandy beaches below, the vulnerability of earth before
the mighty mass of the sea and the heartstrings are touched. Going away from it we are moved, touched.

Tom MacDonagh (1934–): *My Green Age*

***

War

* They proceeded to strike, mangle, slaughter, and cut down one another for a long time, so that men were soon laid low, heroes wounded, youths slain, and robust heroes mangled in the slaughter.

  Annals of the Four Masters: [Shane O'Neill's battle with the O'Donnells, 1567]

* If I live, I mean to spend the rest of my life working for perpetual peace. I have seen war and faced artillery and know what an outrage it is against simple men.

  Thomas Kettle (1880–1916): *Poems and Parodies*

* There is no crime in detecting and destroying in war-time, the spy and the informer. They have destroyed without trial. I have paid them back in their own coin.

  Michael Collins (1890–1922): [Attributed]

* Death comes in quantity from solved
  Problems on maps, well-ordered dispositions,
  Angles of elevation and direction.

  Charles Donnelly (1910–37): 'The Tolerance of Crows'

***

Wisdom & Learning

* Acht chena is álainn cech nderg,
  is gel cach nua, is caín cech n-ard, is serb cech ngáth
  cáid cech n-écmais, is faill cech n-aichnid,
  co festar cech n-éolas.

  But indeed everything red is beautiful, everything new is bright, everything unreachable is lovely, everything familiar is better, everything absent is perfect, everything known is neglected, until all knowledge is known.

  Anonymous (9th century): *The Sick-Bed of Chulainn*

*   Where I am not understood, it shall be concluded that something very useful and profound is couched underneath.

    Jonathan Swift (1667–1745): Preface of *Tale of A Tub*

*   And still they gazed, and still the wonder grew,
    That one small head could carry all he knew.

    Oliver Goldsmith (1728–74): 'The Deserted Village'

*   The only infallible criterion of wisdom to vulgar minds – success.

    Edmund Burke (1729–97): 'Letter to a Member of the National Assembly

*   I often looked up at the sky an' assed meself the question – what is the moon, what is the stars?

    Sean O'Casey (1880–1964): *Juno and the Paycock*

*   Mother: Them that have too much of it [learning] are seven times crosser than them that never saw a book.

    Lady Gregory (1859–1932): *Aristotle Bellows*

*   There's more learning than is taught in books.

    Lady Gregory (1859–1932): *The Jester*

*   I'm walking through the desert
    and I am not frightened although it's hot.
    I have all that I requested
    and do not want what I haven't got.

    Sinéad O'Connor (1966–): 'I do not want what I haven't got'

***

Women

* Atá ben istír,
  Ní abraim a ainm
  maidid essi a deilm
  amal chloich a tailm

  There's a woman in the land
  I won't mention her name–
  And when she breaks wind,
  It's like a stone from a sling.

  Anonymous (8th–12th century)

* Though I have loved twenty men
  This is not what women seek.

  Anonymous (10th century): 'Gormley's Laments'

* They say women and music should never be dated.

  Oliver Goldsmith (1728–74): *She Stoops to Conquer*

* What a misfortune it is to be born a woman! ... Why seek
  for knowledge, which can prove only that our wretched-
  ness is irremediable? If a ray of life break in upon us, it is
  but to make darkness more visible; to show us the new
  limits, the Gothic structure, the impenetrable barriers of
  our prison.

  Maria Edgeworth (1767–1849) : *Leonara*

* The time I've lost in wooing,
  In watching and pursuing
  The light that lies
  In woman's eyes,
  Has been my heart's undoing.
  Though wisdom oft has sought me,
  I scorned the love she bought me,
  My only books
  Were woman's looks,
  And folly's all they've taught me.

  Thomas Moore (1779–1852): 'The Time I've Lost to Wooing'

* Disguise our bondage as we will
  'Tis woman, woman, rules us still.
  Thomas Moore (1779–1852): 'Sovereign Woman'

* We women adore failures. They lean on us.
  Oscar Wilde (1854–1900): *A Woman of No Importance*

* The censors strive with a certain sadness in their hearts,
  for they feel that whatever they do the trouble cannot
  really be removed, only 'regulated' in a haphazard way.
  Woman cannot be abolished, and literature, which finds
  her so dangerously interesting, cannot be suppressed. The
  trouble did not originate in Ireland; it really began with
  'Eve', on whom Irish ecclesiastics preach with extraordi-
  nary feeling and emphasis. If Adam could have sufficed at
  the morning-time of the manifestation of the world! Had
  there been no Eve and no womanhood there would prob-
  ably have been no trouble with literature; nothing in its
  pages would have shocked a curate or brought a blush to
  the brow of the most sensitive bishop. Eve is the eternal
  shadow on the Irish ecclesiastical landscape.
  William Ryan (1867–1942): *Ecclesiastics, Eve and Literature*

* The worker is the slave of the capitalist society, the female
  worker is the slave of that slave.
  James Connolly (1868–1916): *The Reconquest of Ireland*

* Coinnibh an teaghlach geal
  Agus an chlann fé smacht,
  Nigh agus sciór agus glan,
  Cóirigh proinn agus lacht,
  Iompaigh tochta, leag brat,
  Ach, ar nós Sheicheiriseáide,
  Ní mór duit an fhilíocht chomh maith!

  Keep the dwelling bright
  and the children in order;
  wash and scour and clean;

prepare meal and beverage;
turn mattress – spread cloth –
but, like Scheherazade,
you will need to write poetry also.

> Máire Mhac an tSaoi (1922–): 'Cré na Mná Tí'
> ('The Housewife's Credo')

* On the last day of his life Dan decided that women who
haunted you were not those whom you had enjoyed or
even known remotely well, but strangers who had at one
time or another troubled you with the most transient flick-
er of desire.

> Val Mulkerns (1925–): *Loser*

* In particular, the State recognises that by her life within
the home, woman gives to the State a support without
which the common good cannot be achieved.

> The Irish Constitution: [Article 41.2]

* The State acknowledges the right to life of the unborn and,
with due regard to the equal right to life of the mother,
guarantees in its laws to respect, and, as far as practicable,
by its law to defend and vindicate that right.

> The Irish Constitution: [Article 40.3]

* The vote, I thought, means nothing to women. We should
be armed.

> Edna O'Brien (1932–): [Epigraph to *Fear of Flying* by Erica Jong]

* It was my fault. I'm to blame.

> Joan FitzGerald (1930–): [Apologising for the fact that her hus-
> band, leader of the Fine Gael party, appeared in an election
> campaign wearing odd shoes]

* The whole notion of holding a referendum on women's
access to information is such a profound disgrace for a

nation such as this that I ... apologise to Irish women on behalf of what has been predominantly a male-dominated, male-driven male disgrace.

Anthony Clare (1945–): [*The Irish Times*, 8 January 1993]

***

Index of Authors

Index of First Lines

A

B

J

U

W

Y